# Reclaiming Liberalism

AriArmstrong.com

# Reclaiming Liberalism
## and Other Essays on Personal and Economic Freedom

Ari Armstrong

Ember Publishing
Denver, Colorado

Ember Publishing
Denver, Colorado

Armstrong, Ari
Reclaiming Liberalism and Other Essays on Personal
    and Economic Freedom
Includes Index
Political Theory, Government, Current Affairs

Designed by Jennifer Armstrong

ISBN: 978-0-9818030-2-9

For Tomorrow's Liberals

# Contents

# Reclaiming Liberalism

My aim is to reclaim the mantle of liberalism for those who advocate personal and economic freedom, individual rights, and constitutional government that protects rights. This implies that I think there is something amiss with how most Americans today describe themselves politically. We begin there.

What is a conservative? What is a liberal? For most Americans, those labels (among others) adhere to different packages of beliefs.

A conservative, by the usual way of thinking, is someone who leans toward an originalist interpretation of the Constitution; supports relatively free markets, albeit with some trade restrictions and welfare; embraces Judeo-Christian religion; opposes abortion; and accepts a variety of restraints on personal behavior, such as prohibitions of various drugs.

A liberal, by contrast, supports a "living" and malleable Constitution; calls for extensive government regulation of the economy and for large-scale wealth transfers; embraces secular government, with a legal wall separating church and state; favors legal abortion; and accepts a somewhat different set of restraints on personal behavior, such as gun restrictions and "sin" taxes on tobacco and soda.

Conservative thought leaders, Republican candidates, and their fans often spit the word "liberal" as an indictment. Liberal views are what's wrong with the world, and liberals are despicable for promoting those views, goes the line. Liberalism turns "good men into whiners, weenies, and whimps"; it is a "sin" and a "mental disorder" leading to the "demise of America" (to borrow from various book titles). Right-thinking people are not liberals; they are conservatives. Liberalism and conservatism are opposite ends of the political spectrum—corresponding to the political left and right—with moderates in the middle.

Meanwhile, those on the political left (or so regarded today) are happy to embrace the term liberal to describe their views, which they see as corresponding with the so-called Progressivism of the democratic socialist tradition. They, too, see liberals and conservatives as inhabiting opposite ends of the political spectrum, although left-liberals tend to call their opponents "right-wing extremists" and the like. For whatever reason, "conservative" doesn't seem to be as dirty a word for those on today's left as "liberal" is for those on today's right—but conservatism still is eyed with suspicion and disdain.

The problem with such labels as conservative and liberal as typically used is that they group people very roughly by demographic similarities, not by logical coherence of beliefs about ideology and policy.

For example, why do conservatives tend to favor prohibitions of drugs but not of guns? The answer comes mainly not from logic but from anthropology. Conservatives tend to be rural, where rates of gun ownership and hunting are high and where police are distant; and they tend to embrace more fundamentalist sorts of religion, which condemn drunkenness and the like.

On the other hand, why do today's American liberals tend to favor prohibitions of guns but not (always) of drugs? They tend to be more urban, where fewer people legally own guns or hunt. Many urban areas have relatively high rates of violent crime, and the police usually are faster to respond to emergencies. What about drugs? Recall that alcohol Prohibition was a Progressive cause. But today's liberals often focus on the police and incarceration abuses fostered by the drug war. And they tend to be younger and more open to personal experimentation with drugs and the like.

The labels conservative and liberal can be useful in an anthropological consideration of political demographics— particularly as so many Americans self-identify using those terms. The problems come when people mistake anthropological labels for conceptual tools to understand political philosophy.

For many people, the terms conservative and liberal become a cover for intellectual laziness. It's just "obvious" that conservatives believe one set of things while liberals believe another, so why worry much about whether it makes any sense to embrace the elements of a particular package of beliefs?

People who embrace one of today's usual packages of political beliefs often engage in ad hoc rationalization rather than genuine reasoning about those beliefs. For example, self-described conservatives tend to embrace the ideal of self-responsibility— why, then, do many conservatives argue that adults are responsible enough to own an unregistered AR-15 semi-automatic rifle with thirty-round magazines but not to smoke marijuana? Perhaps the conservative would answer that smoking marijuana can reduce a person's capacity for self-responsible action. Well, so can drinking alcohol—and yet hardly any conservative argues for the return of alcohol prohibition. At the same time, many self-described liberals care about the problems of police abuses and needless incarceration caused by drug restrictions while ignoring such problems when caused by gun restrictions—probably because relatively few or their friends and political allies own guns (or at least "scarier" guns).

People who come up with arguments piecemeal to prop up the various elements of their package of beliefs—usually the package that their family or friends embrace—rarely think about whether the elements of the package fit together into a logically coherent whole or about the deeper philosophic grounding of their beliefs.

So why don't we just relegate such terms as conservative and liberal to their anthropological uses and come up with a different set of terms for political philosophy? The answer is that the term liberal, by historical use and by etymological development, is well suited for use as a concept of political philosophy. "Liberal" should mean not only the package of beliefs widely embraced by the self-described liberals of a given era; it should refer to a philosophic worldview that logically implies certain beliefs and policies and not others. As we will see, "conservative" is badly suited to describe a particular political philosophy; nevertheless, we do well to seek a clear, conceptual understanding of the term. The proper goal is to clarify the meaning of the terms liberal and conservative (among others); concocting new terms would increase confusion rather than reduce it.

To think straight we need clear concepts. So let's begin to untangle the meaning and implications of the common terms we use to discuss politics, beginning with liberalism.

## Liberalism Pertains to Liberty

Today in America, many people who call themselves liberals openly endorse censorship of political speech; civilian disarmament by bureaucratic fiat; pervasive violations of freedom of contract, especially involving work; part-time involuntary servitude for the sake of "redistributing" wealth; forced service by business owners for purposes of which they ideologically disapprove; the substantial takeover of education from pre-kindergarten to college by the national government; and a host of other authoritarian measures.

Such people and such policies are not liberal; they are anti-liberal. To effectively advance their cause, true liberals—people who in fact advocate liberty in all affairs, personal and economic— must reclaim the mantle of liberalism. The authoritarians, the statists, the collectivists who stole the term liberalism from its rightful heirs must be stripped of their rhetorical masks and exposed for what they are: enemies of human freedom.

The call to restore liberalism to its historically and etymologically soundest meaning is hardly new. The great liberal (free-market) Austrian economist Ludwig von Mises, before fleeing the Nazis and bringing Carl Menger's school of economics to New York, wrote the book *Liberalismus*—later translated as

*Liberalism*—in 1927.[1] In 1966, Mises discussed his use of the term liberal in his book *Human Action*:

> I employ the term "liberal" in the sense attached to it everywhere in the nineteenth century and still today in countries of continental Europe. This usage is imperative because there is simply no other term available to signify the great political and intellectual movement that substituted free enterprise and the market economy for the precapitalistic methods of production; constitutional representative government for the absolutism of kings or oligarchies; and freedom of all individuals from slavery, serfdom, and other forms of bondage.[2]

Similarly, the Chicago economist Milton Friedman (with whom Mises had important disagreements) embraced the term "liberal," although as a matter of convenience rather than as an "imperative." He writes:

> In the late 18th and early 19th centuries, an intellectual movement developed that went under the name of Liberalism. This development, which was a reaction against the authoritarian elements in the prior society, emphasized freedom as the ultimate goal and the individual as the ultimate entity in the society. It supported *laissez faire* at home as a means of reducing the role of the state in economic affairs and thereby avoiding interfering with the individual; it supported free trade abroad as a means of linking the nations of the world together peacefully and democratically. In political matters, it supported

---

1   Bettina Bien Greaves, "Preface, 1985," in Ludwig von Mises, *Liberalism in the Classical Tradition* (San Francisco: Cobden Press, 1985), p. v.

2   Ludwig von Mises, *Human Action*, Third Revised Edition (Chicago: Henry Regnery Company, 1966), p. v. Jeffrey Tucker also mentions this passage in "Take Back the Word 'Liberal,'" Foundation for Economic Education, January 2, 2015, https://fee.org/articles/take-back-the-word-liberal/.

the development of representative government and of parliamentary institutions, reduction in the arbitrary power of the state, and protection of the civil freedoms of individuals.[3]

However, in the 20th Century, Friedman continues, the term "liberal" began to mean advocacy for coercive transfers of wealth ("welfare") and government intervention in people's affairs to achieve such transfers. Friedman continues:

> This use of the term liberalism in these two quite different senses renders it difficult to have a convenient label for the principles I shall be talking about. I shall resolve these difficulties by using the word liberalism in its original sense. Liberalism of what I have called the 20th century variety has by now become orthodox and indeed reactionary. Consequently, the views I shall present might equally be entitled, under current conditions, the "new liberalism," a more attractive designation than "nineteenth century liberalism."

Liberalism is best understood to mean devotion to and advocacy of human liberty. Today's true champions of liberty and true heirs of the liberal tradition need to put an end to the widespread perversion of the term by the anti-liberals who now claim it.

Advocates of liberty should reclaim liberalism for three basic reasons.

First, historically, the term liberal in a political context most prominently describes the broad movement that, in the main, advocates freedom in economic and personal affairs, grounded in

---

3  Milton Friedman, "Capitalism and Freedom," in *New Individualist Review* (Indianapolis, Indiana: Liberty Fund, 1981), http://oll.libertyfund.org/titles/2136 #NIR_1360-001_head_009. Originally this was published by Intercollegiate Society of Individualists, April 1961, vol. 1, no. 1. Friedman makes comparable statements in his book *Capitalism and Freedom*, Fortieth Anniversary Edition (University of Chicago Press, 2002), pp. 5–6.

a (broadly) Lockean theory of individual rights and representative government.

Second, etymologically, the term liberal relates to being free or unbridled.[4] True, "liberal" can also refer to generosity (roughly, free in offering aid) and freedom from prejudice. But these alternate meanings do not buttress today's authoritarian "liberalism." Generously spending one's own resources is hardly on par with generously spending the resources of others. Presuming that elements of economic liberty arose from prejudicial beliefs is to begin with one's conclusions rather than to prove them. I would argue that liberalism, in the sense of freedom in economic and personal affairs, encompasses consensual generosity and overturns the prejudices of humankind's authoritarian past.

Third, by appropriating the term liberal, the authoritarians left the advocates of (broadly) Lockean liberty ("free minds and free markets," as *Reason* magazine summarizes it) without a good term of their own. It's not as though these statists needed another term: They already appropriated "socialism" to mean social coercion and "Progressivism" to mean (democratic) socialism—which genuine liberals regard as deeply regressive. Neither the term conservative nor libertarian aptly describes the ideological movement properly called liberal (for reasons considered below). By allowing statists to co-opt the term liberal, liberals of the Lockean tradition largely erased themselves from modern discourse. People have a hard time thinking about that for which they lack a good conceptual term.

Today, the most "obvious" alternative to statist "liberalism" is conservatism. But, not only is today's conservatism often at odds with (Lockean) liberalism, it is not even a coherent political philosophy in its own right. Let us take a closer look.

---

4   "Liberal," *Online Etymological Dictionary*, http://www.etymonline.com/index .php?term=liberal (accessed July 31, 2016).

## The Incoherence of Conservatism

As an ideology, conservatism ultimately is incoherent. Conservatism makes sense only with respect to a particular and specified historical tradition; to oppose any and all change as an end in itself is to embrace stupidity, not an ideology. A delimited conservatism necessarily sanctions the ideological roots of the tradition it seeks to conserve; hence, conservatism is not an ideology, but rather a commitment to some particular ideology implied by or manifest in some tradition. So a conservative, depending on particulars, might favor monarchic rule over revolution, American constitutionalism over "living constitution" Progressivism, slavery over abolition, or religious tradition over secularization (as a few examples).

Conservatism cannot be salvaged as a coherent ideology in its own right by taking it to mean favoring "institutions and practices that have evolved gradually and are manifestations of continuity and stability" (as the *Encyclopaedia Britannica* has it).[5] Such an interpretation has two basic problems.

First, in almost all places and times, multiple traditions coexist, so to conserve one line of tradition often means to rebel against another. So, for example, when the tradition of slavery butts heads against the (newer) tradition of individual rights, which shall the conservative conserve? In many cases, conservatism is but an intellectually sloppy way to rationalize the embrace of one tradition over another while leaving deeper reasons or motivations shrouded. The attitude often seems to be, "What reasons need I? I'm a conservative." By the same token, one who looks hard enough can place any proposed change within the boundaries of some tradition or other, often going back to the ancient Greeks or further. Both the Nazis and their enemies could claim the conservative mantle, as could both the slavers and the abolitionists.

---

5   Richard Dagger, "Conservatism," *Encyclopaedia Britannica*, May 25, 2016, https://www.britannica.com/topic/conservatism.

Second, there is no such thing as consistently gradual evolution of human institutions over sufficiently long periods of time, so conservatives necessarily embrace whatever radical changes transpired in the tradition they seek to uphold. Do Christian conservatives deny that their religion was at its founding radical, and that its widespread embrace led to profound and relatively fast social change? Do Constitutionalists deny that the American Revolution was a radical response to monarchic abuse, resulting in far-reaching social upheaval? Scratch a conservative, find a revolutionary—if you take a given tradition back far enough.

To continue this last point, one problem with conservatism is that any revolutionary can claim to be a conservative; there is no change so dramatic that its defenders can't frame it neatly within some tradition. By any sensible reading, Christianity is radically different from the religion of the Torah. Yet Jesus (through his biographers) cast himself as a conservative: "I have come [not] to abolish the Law or the Prophets . . . but to fulfill them" (Matthew 5:17).

So too were America's revolutionary Founders conservatives by their own lights. They weren't upheaving the existing order; they were merely obeying "the Laws of Nature and of Nature's God"—what could be more conservative than that? The Founders acknowledged the imprudence of overthrowing a government "for light and transient causes," yet saw the move as necessary in their case due to the monarch's pervasive abuses. To adapt Jesus's words, the Founders came not to abolish English legal traditions, but to fulfill them.

If Jesus and America's Founders can be conservatives, then anyone can be a conservative. Even Marx can be considered a conservative, in that he casts every movement of history as the culmination of previous movements. Conservatism becomes a tool—a trick, really—to pacify those who romanticize the past.

Every moment in history is partly new, partly rooted in the past. Every moment is at once a revolution and a conservation. To insist that a given incident is one rather than the other usually is not very helpful. Noticing what changes and what stays the same can be more helpful. There is no firm line separating fast change from slow; rather, speed of change lies on a continuum. Ancient Egyptian society stayed largely the same for long periods of time; the Enlightenment and the resulting Industrial Revolution resulted in breathtakingly rapid changes. (Which does the American conservative prefer?) But Egypt was not completely unaffected by the passing of time, and the Enlightenment was not an absolute break with the past. At most, the sensible conservative can say, "This is the wrong type of change," or, "We should proceed relatively slowly in this given case."

In many cases, a person calls himself a conservative to avoid saying precisely what he is for, and why. To imply that you are right because your view is the traditional one is to evade the essential questions. Which traditions do you support, which traditions do you oppose, which innovations do you support, which meddlings do you oppose—and why? A conservative without deeper reasons for his positions is a fraud or a huckster; a conservative with reasons is not, fundamentally, a conservative.

## Conservatism, Utopianism, and Liberalism

Conservatives erroneously think that they alone stand against utopianism and that liberalism tends toward utopianism. In fact, genuine liberalism rejects utopianism (literally, no place)—despite the fact that some utopians are also confused about this. A political philosophy fancied as liberal by its advocates is not, in fact, liberal, if it aims at some imaginary version of liberty while undercutting the basis of the real thing.

The great economist Friedrich Hayek (who was strongly influenced by Mises) hesitated to call himself a liberal because "American radicals and socialists began calling themselves 'liberals,'" and "in Europe the predominant type of rationalistic liberalism has long been one of the pacemakers of socialism."[6] Hayek, then, feared that one strain of liberalism tended toward socialist utopianism.

In railing against "rationalistic liberalism," Hayek points to ideologies that ignore the importance of institutions (particularly those of government), ignore realities of human nature, and seek instead to achieve a "liberty" unmoored from reality. Hayek worries that such utopian ideologies sully the tradition of liberalism; I counter that they are not truly part of that tradition, but opposed to it.

Following Hayek, Jonah Goldberg too rails against utopian "liberalism."[7] Indeed, he suggests that the socialist variants of "liberalism" are what keep him from embracing the mantle of liberalism. He says that "progressives stole the label" liberal. He grants, "The American Founding, warts and all, was the apotheosis of classical liberalism, and conservatism here has always been about preserving it." Paraphrasing Hayek, he says that only in America could "one . . . be a conservative and a defender of the liberal tradition." He continues:

> I have no problem with people who say that American conservatism is simply classical liberalism. As a shorthand, that's fine by me. But philosophically, I'm not sure this does the trick. There are many, many, rooms in the mansion of classical liberalism and not all of them are, properly speaking, conservative.

Remarkably, Goldberg, writing for the flagship conservative publication *National Review*, here is saying that he *is* a (classical) liberal—a conservative liberal.

---

6   Friedrich Hayek, "Why I Am Not a Conservative," in *The Constitution of Liberty* (University of Chicago Press, 1960), republished by the Cato Institute at http:// object.cato.org/sites/cato.org/files/articles/hayek-why-i-am-not-conservative.pdf (accessed July 18, 2016).

7   Jonah Goldberg, "When We Say 'Conservative,' We Mean . . . ," *National Review*, June 20, 2015, http://www.nationalreview.com/g-file/420055/when-we -say-conservative-we-mean-jonah-goldberg.

But a careful look at Goldberg's defense of a uniquely conservative sort of liberalism reveals that he doesn't really have a defense. Rather, he contrasts his conservative liberalism with (illiberal) utopian fantasies such as anarcho-capitalism and with (illiberal) views that are not "grounded in reality," not attuned to human flourishing, and the like. He fails to capture any ground for a specifically conservative subset of liberalism.

Liberalism properly understood necessarily includes a respect for human nature, an understanding of institutions, and due concern about unintended consequences of social change—things that Goldberg sees as conservative. A "liberalism" without such qualities achieves not liberty but chaos, oppression, and tyranny. Without its careful attention to the institutions of government—particularly the checks and balances needed to hinder political fads, demagogues, and democratic madness—the revolutionary era would not have been the "apotheosis of classical liberalism."

Genuine liberalism necessarily excludes utopianism; it is inherently conservative in certain respects. So, properly understood, the "conservative" in "conservative liberal" is not a qualifier narrowing the concept; it is an emphasis of certain necessary aspects of liberalism.

But Goldberg and American conservatives generally are not content to find the conservatism inherent in liberalism. Rather, they seek to stitch liberal views with illiberal ones and name this Frankenstein's monster conservatism.

Consider how often conservatives eagerly sacrifice liberty in the name of religion, tradition, or popular will. People should be free—but not to decide which drugs to consume. Government should protect freedom of expression—and ban certain forms of pornography involving consenting adults. People should be free to trade with others, unimpeded—but not with foreigners. Employers should be free to hire whom they please—except for Mexicans. People should be protected equally under the law—unless they are gay and wish to marry. People should be free to decide how to spend their money—unless the government or some social welfare program really needs it. People generally should be free to live their own lives—except government should force women to carry a just-fertilized zygote to term. (These are all typical but not universal conservative views; for example, Goldberg is "very sympathetic to arguments for gay marriage.")[8]

Among less-intellectual politicians and activists, conservatism often becomes an excuse to pragmatically embrace a huge array of statist measures, including expanded government controls of medicine (RomneyCare), corporate bailouts, massive welfare programs, tariffs, subsidies (Marco Rubio as sugar's sugardaddy), and myriad business regulations. In effect, conservatism becomes a license to cheat on Lady Liberty at will.

## Liberalism as Radical and Rational

Liberalism proper is radical, not utopian. It is an alternative to statist, tradition-bound conservatism as well as to socialism and other forms of "progressive" statism.

Radical means "root" or "change from the roots."[9] To be radical means to get to the roots of one's ideas. Radicalism comes in many stripes. A radical might be a Marxist, a totalitarian Muslim, an ascetic Christian, a pacifist, or a nationalist (as examples). "Radical" refers not to the content of ideas, but rather to taking one's ideas seriously and seeking to understand those ideas fully and implement them. So a radical liberal—one who takes individual rights seriously and advocates rights-protecting government—should not be confused with a radical who embraces a conflicting ideology, such as socialism. (Ultimately, I would argue that only rational ideas can be truly radical, rooted in sense perception and logic, but that qualification need not further concern us here.)

8  Jonah Goldberg, "Gay Marriage Vs. Goodwill," *USA Today*, April 1, 2013, http://www.usatoday.com/story/opinion/2013/04/01/goldberg-gay-marriage-vs-goodwill/2043429/.

9  See "Radical," *Online Etymology Dictionary*, http://www.etymonline.com/index.php?term=radical (accessed August 2, 2016).

A liberal is a radical insofar as he seeks to dig down to the deepest theoretical roots supporting individual rights and representative government. For example, Ayn Rand, who used the term capitalism to refer to the socio-economic system of individual rights and free markets (i.e., liberalism), said of those who advocate her beliefs, "[We] are not 'conservatives.' We are radicals for capitalism; we are fighting for that philosophical base which capitalism did not have and without which it was doomed to perish."[10]

A radical liberal tends to look fundamentally to reason, not faith or tradition, for guidance; in this sense, liberalism is the opposite of conservatism. Although the modern conception of individual rights has roots deep in history, in the main it is a product of the reason-centered Enlightenment. Liberalism's reliance on reason is precisely why conservatives distrust it—but they are wrong to do so.

Conservatives worry that, because liberalism is rooted in reason, it inherently tends toward "scientific" socialism. Just look at the mass-murdering, atheistic socialist regimes of the Twentieth Century, conservatives urge. Here we needn't get deeply into the matter that Marx, the Young Hegelian who modified his predecessor's delusional metaphysical rantings, was not actually an advocate of reason. As C. Bradley Thompson summarizes, far from embracing evidence-based reason, "Marxism represents a revolt against the laws of reality."[11] For our purposes, the key point is that liberalism rejects rationalist socialism and shares essentially nothing in common with it. ("Rationalism" here refers, not to

---

10   Ayn Rand, "Conservatives," *Ayn Rand Lexicon*, http://aynrandlexicon.com/lexicon/conservatives.html (accessed August 2, 2016).
11   C. Bradley Thompson, "Why Marxism—Evil Laid Bare," *Objective Standard*, Summer 2012, vol. 7, no. 2, https://www.theobjectivestandard.com/issues/2012-summer/why-marxism/.

evidence-based reason, but to superficially logical arguments detached from reality.)[12]

Liberalism rejects the collectivist notion that allegedly "rational planners" can, for the "good of society," coercively run people's lives or the economy as a whole. Such "planners" in reality are pervasively ignorant about people's values and about how people accomplish their goals, and they typically lack the incentives to plan well even if they could do so. As Mises eloquently explains, such centralized, allegedly rational planning actually impedes or destroys people's ability to rationally plan their own lives. True, a liberal order leaves individuals free to run their lives rationally or not. But if individuals choose to live by reason, government does not stop them; and if they do not, government does not force others to engage with them.

Genuine liberalism is radical, not rash; rational, not unmoored from reality. Conservatives and others are wrong to conflate liberalism with socialism. Radical liberals understand and feed the roots of liberty; rationalist socialists uproot the plant.

I think for our purposes here I've adequately outlined the relationship between liberalism and conservatism. Next, it will be helpful to see how liberalism fits with other common political terms, starting with left and right.

## The Problem with Left and Right

Americans tend to use "left" as a synonym for Progressive or socialist tendencies and "right" for conservative and free market ones.

In addition to the fact that conservatives often oppose free markets, an obvious problem immediately asserts itself: "Right" often also refers to (socialistic) fascists and to (collectivist) racists.

---

12   For a detailed discussion of rationalism, see Leonard Peikoff, *Understanding Objectivism* (New York: New American Library, 2012), edited by Michael S. Berliner, especially the sections "Rationalism," "Rationalism and Empiricism," and "Objectivism Versus Rationalism and Empiricism."

But the "right-wing" views of genuine liberals are antithetical to the views of "right-wing" fascists and racists.[13]

A term that packages together such disparate and contradictory things sows more confusion than clarity. Undoubtedly Marxists (and their fellow travelers) will claim that liberal capitalism tends toward fascism and racial nationalism, but that's nonsense. Liberalism embraces local and international free trade, calls for rights-respecting government, and demands equality under the law. Packaging it with racism and nationalist socialism is dishonest and absurd. Hence, it makes no sense to distinguish "center right" from "far right" as the terms currently are used; there can be no continuum of fundamentally unlike things.

I do think that ideological movements of the left (as understood today) have something in common—statism, meaning (roughly) advocacy of government controls and wealth transfers. So there is a continuum of socialist-left politics, and "center left" is less statist than "far left." For example, the "left-wing" Scandinavian welfare states do have *something* in common with the murderous and oppressive "left-wing" Soviet regime—the forced transfer of wealth—but the differences are far more pronounced. So, unlike the term right-wing as it is usually used, the term left-wing at least has a coherent meaning.

Replacing the term leftist with statist would be much more descriptive of what we're actually talking about. When I use the term statist, I do mean it pejoratively, but that's because I think that statism is wrong. In the same way, I've used leftist pejoratively. Today's leftists should have no more problem embracing the statist label—Barack Obama and Hillary Clinton loudly brag about using the state to "invest in the economy" and the like—than I have embracing the capitalist label, in its origins a pejorative term for a free economy.

---

13  Ayn Rand, for example, harshly condemned racism and fascism. See Ayn Rand, "Racism," in *The Virtue of Selfishness* (New York: Signet Books, 1964); and "Fascism and Communism/Socialism," *Ayn Rand Lexicon*, http://aynrandlexicon.com/lexicon/fascism_and_communism-socialism.html (accessed September 13, 2016).

So the statists are on one side, in my scheme; the liberals are on the other. If statists don't like that term, I suggest that's because they wish to obscure the nature of their political beliefs.

A qualifier: I use statism to refer to advocacy of government action above and beyond the protection of individual rights. To anarchists, I too am a statist because I advocate a rights-respecting government, not the abolition of government. But there is an important difference between a government that acts only to protect individual rights and a government that acts to transfer wealth and control peaceable people. Theorists such as Mises and Rand have long used the term statism as I do here.

There is another problem with the way that most people use left and right today: It does not mesh well with the historical uses of those terms. Originally, the terms referred to the seating of French politicians in 1789: Those on the right favored the established order; those on the left, revolution. Originally a "leftist" was closer to a liberal (as I use the term) than to a socialist.[14]

Yet a liberal shares some of the concerns of those on the traditional right. Max Forrester Eastman suggests that, originally, a leftist "stood for the individual and his liberties" while a rightist backed the "constituted authorities."[15] Well, if the constituted authority is a tyrannical monarchy, then a liberal is against it. But a liberal is not against authority per se, as when police lawfully arrest someone suspected of murder. The liberal embraces both liberty and lawful authority. Indeed, the rights of the individual can be protected only by a rights-respecting government with due authority to fulfill its mandate; properly, individual rights and government authority go hand in hand. So, in this sense, a liberal

---

14   On this point, see Leonard E. Read, "Neither Left nor Right," Foundation for Economic Education, January 1, 2006, https://fee.org/articles/neither-left-nor-right/. The essay originally is from 1956.

15   Max Forrester Eastman, "What to Call Yourself," Foundation for Economic Education, July 8, 2016, https://fee.org/articles/what-to-call-yourself/. The essay originally is from 1953.

represents the union of left and right, of individual liberty and a government authorized to protect it, rather than a choice of one or a rejection of both. Liberalism flies with both these wings and cannot fly without them.

Can the terms right and left be salvaged by redefining them? Craig Biddle of the *Objective Standard* (for which I used to write) plausibly argues that we should use "right" to refer to what I'm calling liberal and "left" to refer to statist. But his case seems contrived; he says that "the right" corresponds with the term rights (as in individual rights) and that the protection of rights is "morally right."[16] Biddle makes the terms coherent, but I think the term right-wing has become too muddied for him to salvage it. Biddle now uses the term "liberal right,"[17] which is fine, although ultimately I think it is better to drop out the term "right" and fully reclaim the term liberal.

For now, given how widespread the use of the terms left and right are, I propose to continue using the terms where useful, but only with qualifiers or context that clarifies the intended meaning (such as Biddle's "liberal right"). The term "statist left" clearly refers to advocacy of government force (beyond the protection of rights). "Civil liberties left" refers to the genuinely liberal tradition of upholding freedom of speech and the like. The newly popular terms "illiberal left," "regressive left," and "authoritarian left" aptly describe the movement that seeks to squash political

---

16  Craig Biddle, "Political 'Left' and 'Right' Properly Defined," *Objective Standard*, June 26, 2012, https://www.theobjectivestandard.com/2012/06/political-left-and -right-properly-defined/.

17  Craig Biddle, "Liberal Right vs. Regressive Left and Religious 'Right,'" *Objective Standard*, July 12, 2016, https://www.theobjectivestandard.com/2016/07/liberal -right-vs-regressive-left-and-religious-right/. Incidentally, I tried out the term "free-market liberal" in the same journal; see Ari Armstrong, "Why I'm a Free-Market Liberal," *Objective Standard*, August 11, 2012, https://www.theobjectivestandard .com/2012/08/why-im-a-free-market-liberal/.

debate (especially on college campuses) and to excuse horrific acts of select groups (especially totalitarian jihadists).[18]

What is critically important is that we stop using the terms right and left to package together contradictory ideas, such as economic liberty and racism ("right") or freedom of speech and an intrusive state ("left"). The true liberal is neither left nor right, if those terms refer to collectivist socialism and racial fascism, or both left and right, if they refer to individual liberties and properly constituted government.

## The Long-Term Reclamation of Liberalism

Obviously, genuine liberals cannot just go around in modern America, proclaim themselves liberals without any context, and expect people to understand what they're talking about. For too many decades people have abused the term.

Liberals should declare themselves to be such in order to reclaim the name of their political beliefs and to help clarify people's language and thinking. But liberals need to proclaim their liberalism with relevant qualifiers and context, until such time as the term is broadly understood to mean what its etymology and history imply.

Consider some examples of sensible liberal answers to inquiries about political views:

"I'm a liberal in the classical sense, meaning I advocate individual rights, free markets, and constitutional government."

"If 'left' refers to individual freedom and 'right' refers to tradition and law and order, then in a way I'm both. I advocate America's tradition of constitutional government for the protection of individual rights. But if left means socialism and right means fascism or racial nationalism, then I reject both."

---

18   For an example of the use of such terminology, see Maajid Nawaz, "The British Left's Hypocritical Embrace of Islamism," *Daily Beast*, August 8, 2015, http://www .thedailybeast.com/articles/2015/08/08/the-british-left-s-hypocritical-embrace-of -islamism.html.

"People who usually call themselves liberals today are nothing of the sort. They are statists, not liberals. They advocate rights-violating government that confiscates people's wealth and controls their lives. That's not liberal and progressive; it's illiberal and regressive. I'm a genuine liberal; I advocate individual liberty."

"Liberalism properly understood is neither about the isolated individual nor about a society that crushes individual rights and values. Rather, it refers to a system in which individuals freely pursue their values in voluntary association with others, in accordance with others' equal rights."

I have now made the essential case for reclaiming liberalism, and I have described the basics of how to accomplish the reclamation. Yet there is one more matter I need to address: Why not embrace the newer term libertarian? After all, my policy views overlap substantially with those of self-described libertarians. Wouldn't it be easier just to buy into the libertarian label than to reclaim the term liberal? No; libertarianism is not liberalism, and it is a mistake for liberals to call themselves libertarians.

## Why Not Libertarianism?

"Libertarian" is by now a widely recognized term that means, loosely, "socially liberal and fiscally conservative." The 2016 Libertarian presidential candidate Gary Johnson helped popularize this sort of description.[19] But such language embeds the sorts of confusions discussed above. Does "socially liberal" imply that government should punish businesses that discriminate against homosexuals, as Johnson endorses?[20] Does "fiscally conservative" mean support for tariffs, corporate

---

19  For example, see Clare Malone, "Gary Johnson Is Here to Tell You You're a Libertarian," *FiveThirtyEight*, June 10, 2016, http://fivethirtyeight.com/features/gary-johnson-is-here-to-tell-you-youre-a-libertarian/.

20  Kyle Sammin, "Think Twice before Voting for Gary Johnson as a Trump Protest Vote," *Federalist*, May 19, 2016, http://thefederalist.com/2016/05/19/think-twice-before-voting-for-gary-johnson-as-a-trump-protest-vote/.

subsidies, and a welfare state, as it does for many self-described conservatives? If we take "fiscally conservative" to mean free-market in some sense, then economic liberty is presumed by Johnson's language to be outside of liberalism rather than a part of it. In such ways libertarianism confuses the discussion rather than clarifies it.

As some people describe it, libertarianism just is liberalism. For example, David Boaz of the flagship libertarian think tank the Cato Institute lists a package of "libertarian" beliefs including individualism, individual rights, the rule of law, and free markets.[21] Apparently part of the idea is that the term liberal has been so corrupted that it's easier to use the newer term libertarian instead. But it is a tactical mistake to continue to cede the term liberal to anti-liberals, as doing so keeps alive the usual confusions.

There is a much deeper problem: Libertarianism does not just mean liberalism; it means most prominently an antagonism toward government as such. Perhaps this remark will seem surprising to self-described libertarians who admit the need for (some) government. My claim is not that all libertarians are anarchists; rather it is that libertarianism tends to foster animosity toward government, and, ultimately, it tends toward anarchy.

As an indication of the problem, consider that Jeffrey Tucker, an outspoken anarchist (and in many respects otherwise a wonderful writer), is (as of late 2016) the Director of Content for the Foundation for Economic Education, an important free-market institution since 1946. Tucker, too, wishes to reclaim the term liberal—for anarchists. He says that "genuine liberalism has continued to learn and grow and now finds a more consistent embodiment in what is often but awkwardly called *libertarianism*

---

21 David Boaz, "Key Concepts of Libertarianism," Cato Institute, January 1, 1999, http://www.cato.org/publications/commentary/key-concepts-libertarianism.

or *market anarchism*, both of which are rightly considered an extension of the old liberal intellectual project."[22]

The Institute for Humane Studies, an organization that sponsors numerous libertarian events (some of which I've attended and enjoyed), likewise wants to extend liberalism to anarchism:

> The libertarian or "classical liberal" perspective is that peace, prosperity, and social harmony are fostered by "as much liberty as possible" and "as little government as necessary." . . . Libertarian is not a single viewpoint, but includes a wide variety of perspectives. Libertarians can range from market anarchists to advocates of a limited welfare state, but they are all united by a belief in personal liberty, economic freedom, and a skepticism of government power.[23]

Here we get the idea of what it typically means to be a libertarian: It is either to embrace anarchy outright or else to grudgingly think that some given level of government is practically "necessary," despite the theoretical ideal of no government. Some libertarians think government can feasibly be reduced only to a modest welfare state; others think it can be abolished. The sentiment remains that government is inherently bad, to be tolerated only if it must be. Libertarians tend to equate freedom with the absence of government, and libertarians are more "pure" the more government they're willing to cut. The main concern for libertarianism is how much government there is.

---

22  Jeffrey A. Tucker, "Take Back the Word 'Liberal,'" Foundation for Economic Education, January 2, 2015, https://fee.org/articles/take-back-the-word-liberal/. Tucker also uses libertarian as a synonym for liberal; see Jeffrey Tucker, "Where Does the Term 'Libertarian' Come From Anyway?," Foundation for Economic Education, September 15, 2016, https://fee.org/articles/where-does-the-term-libertarian-come -from-anyway/.

23  "What Is Libertarian," Institute for Humane Studies, https://theihs.org/home/ who-we-are/what-is-libertarian/ (accessed August 14, 2016).

But the absence of government does not mean the presence of liberty. On the contrary, a rights-respecting government is necessary for liberty. Mises rightly rejects the notion that the best government is that "which governs least." Instead, he points out, "Government ought to do all the things for which it is needed and for which it was established. Government ought to protect the individuals within the country against the violent and fraudulent attacks of gangsters, and it should defend the country against foreign enemies."[24] So the proper measure of good government is not its size, however that is calculated; rather, it is that it serves its proper purpose of protecting rights. If a government faces large-scale foreign aggression or widespread internal violence, as examples, it properly expands in size such that it can address the problems at hand.

To the genuine liberal, smaller government is not necessarily better. A government that inadequately addresses crime or that inadequately adjudicates property disputes (for example) is too small, and it should seek greater resources to accomplish such tasks.[25]

Although anarchism is in my view a fundamentally anti-liberal position, I am not arguing that libertarians, including explicitly anarchist ones, should not be included in the liberal tradition. Many of today's top libertarian scholars, including economist Bryan Caplan and philosopher Michael Huemer, are anarchists, but they are not only anarchists. They often do pathbreaking work in a variety of fields supportive of the broadly liberal project. They are liberals despite their anarchism, not because of it.

24    Ludwig von Mises, *Economic Policy: Thoughts for Today and Tomorrow* (Indianapolis, Indiana: Liberty Fund, 1979), edited by Bettina Bien Greaves, http://oll.libertyfund.org/titles/mises-economic-policy-thoughts-for-today-and-tomorrow.

25    See Eric Daniels's excellent discussion of this matter in "Why 'Big Government' is Not the Problem," *Objective Standard*, Spring 2013, vol. 8, no. 1, https://www.theobjectivestandard.com/issues/2013-spring/why-big-government-is-not-the-problem/.

Of course, the so-called anarcho-capitalists (and I used to count myself as both an anarchist and a libertarian) will continue to argue that anarchism ultimately is the truest form of liberalism. I'm not going to further pursue that debate here; I will contend only that the distinction is important enough that liberals who think properly constituted government is necessary for the protection of rights ought not count themselves as libertarians.

History also poses a challenge for those who would use libertarianism to mean liberalism. In its roots the term was much more closely associated with socialist movements than with free-market ones. As Noam Chomsky observes, "The term libertarian as used in the US means something quite different from what it meant historically and still means in the rest of the world. Historically, the libertarian movement has been the anti-statist wing of the socialist movement. Socialist anarchism was libertarian socialism."[26]

Given the myriad problems with the term libertarian, and the obvious advantages of the term liberal to describe an order based on individual rights, liberalism clearly wins the day.

## Renewing the Fight for Liberty

Today's debate between "liberals" (as usually understood) and conservatives is profoundly confused. Very often, that "debate" revolves around which form of statism to more fully embrace. The detestable 2016 presidential election with its two major-party statists is merely an indicator of the broader trend.

Liberalism (real liberalism) is a movement worth saving. Liberals recognize the moral right of individual to pursue their own lives and values, free from the coercion of others. Liberals recognize the need for properly constituted government to protect people's rights equally. Liberals embrace the economic

---

26  Phillip Smith, "Noam Chomsky on the Drug-Terror Link," *Alternet*, February 13, 2002, http://www.alternet.org/story/12420/noam_chomsky_on_the_drug-terror_link.

progress made possible by free-market capitalism. Liberals call for human relationships based on mutual consent, not force. Liberals recognize the magnificent achievement of the United States government—and seek to more fully realize its promise of liberty.

It is time for those of us who advocate liberty to get our voice back, to get our name back, to once again proudly proclaim that we are liberals.

# The Irrationality of
# Neil deGrasse Tyson's Rationalia

IF ONLY SOCIETY COULD BE GOVERNED by a rational elite, what a wonderful world it would be. Or at least various theorists have speculated since Plato penned the *Republic*.

Astrophysicist and science popularizer Neil deGrasse Tyson is the latest in a long line of utopian theorists. He set off a spirited debate when, on June 29, he Tweeted: "Earth needs a virtual country: #Rationalia, with a one-line Constitution: All policy shall be based on the weight of evidence."[27]

Apparently at least some people found the idea appealing; over ten thousand people retweeted the remark, and over twenty-four thousand "liked" it. Of course, Tyson's remark also drew pointed criticism. Robert F. Graboyes, Jeffrey Guhin, S. Shane

---

27 Neil deGrasse Tyson, June 29, 2016, https://twitter.com/neiltyson/status/748 157273789300736.

Morris, Kevin D. Williamson, Kelsey D. Atherton, Jesse Singal, and David Roberts are among those who criticized Tyson.[28]

The main thrust of the criticisms of Tyson, with which I heartily agree, is that self-proclaimed "rational" people very often, in fact, are not rational. Just consider how widespread eugenics was among the scientific elite not too many decades ago.

Another problem is that the natural sciences that Tyson invokes do not, by themselves, generally imply particular political conclusions, and thinking they do is hubris. For example, biology can tell us many interesting things about the fetus at various stages of development; it cannot, however, tell us whether or how to restrict abortion. And, as Roberts points out, the scientific facts about climate change do not, by themselves, tell us what we should do about it. (Alex Epstein plausibly argues we should respond to climate change by using more fossil fuels.)[29]

---

28  Robert F. Graboyes, "The Rationalia Fallacy," *U.S. News & World Report*, July 18, 2016, http://www.usnews.com/opinion/articles/2016-07-18/neil-degrasse-tyson-may-dream-of-a-rationalia-society-but-its-a-fallacy; Jeffrey Guhin, "A Nation Ruled by Science Is a Terrible Idea," *Slate*, July 5, 2016, http://www.slate.com/articles/health_and_science/science/2016/07/neil_degrasse_tyson_wants_a_nation_ruled_by_evidence_but_evidence_explains.html; G. Shane Morris, "Neil DeGrasse Tyson's 'Rationalia' Would Be A Terrible Country," *Federalist*, July 1, 2016, http://thefederalist.com/2016/07/01/neil-degrasse-tysons-rationalia-would-be-a-terrible-country/; Kevin D. Williamson, "The Road to Rationalia," *National Review*, June 30, 2016, http://www.nationalreview.com/article/437324/neil-degrasse-tysons-rationality-pipe-dream; Kelsey D. Atherton, "Neil deGrasse Tyson's Proposed 'Rationalia' Government Won't Work," *Popular Science*, June 29, 2016, http://www.popsci.com/neil-degrasse-tyson-just-proposed-government-that-doesnt-work; Kelsey D. Atherton, "Neil deGrasse Tyson Doubles Down on Rationalia," *Popular Science*, August 8, 2016, http://www.popsci.com/neil-degrasse-tyson-doubles-down-on-rationalia; Jesse Singal, "Neil DeGrasse Tyson's Viral Tweet About Starting a New Country Is Bad and Useful," *Science of Us*, June 30, 2016, http://nymag.com/scienceofus/2016/06/neil-degrasse-tysons-viral-tweet-about-starting-a-new-country-is-bad-and-useful.html; David Roberts, "3 questions for Neil deGrasse Tyson," *Vox*, June 30, 2016, http://www.vox.com/2016/6/30/12064540/3-questions-for-neil-degrasse-tyson.

29  See Alex Epstein, *The Moral Case for Fossil Fuels* (New York: Penguin, 2014).

Then there is the critical problem of who gets to decide who is sufficiently rational to be in charge. Who watches the watchers, who guards the guardians? People tried to create real-world Rationalias in the Twentieth Century, several times. Communism was supposed to be about rationally and scientifically planning the economy. Not only did this lead to allegedly rational planners governing by profound ignorance, causing widespread devastation; it led to despicable people taking charge. The Communists committed the worst mass murders in history in terms of number of victims, followed by the (allegedly also rational) National-Socialist German Workers' Party.[30] Socialist versions of Rationalia failed repeatedly and spectacularly.

Arch-skeptic Michael Shermer suggests the obvious cure for the problem of guarding the guardians: Set up government institutions that foster rational outcomes. Shermer is much more sensitive to the importance of government institutions than Tyson seems to be. He claims that "Rationalia already exists"; it is "the Enlightenment experiment running here since 1776."[31] It is the experiment of representative democracy, he adds, which further allows policy experimentation.[32]

Certainly the Founders strove to be rational in setting up the United States government, looking to the guide of history and to the requirements of human nature. For example, as *Federalist* 51 points out, "A dependence on the people is, no doubt, the primary control on the government; but experience has taught

---

30  Ilya Somin, "Remembering the Biggest Mass Murder in the History of the World," *Washington Post*, August 3, 2016, https://www.washingtonpost.com/news/volokh-conspiracy/wp/2016/08/03/giving-historys-greatest-mass-murderer-his-due/?utm_term=.ac9ac4e09f80.

31  Michael Shermer, August 7, 2016, https://twitter.com/michaelshermer/status/762470609414529024.

32  Michael Shermer, August 9, 2016, https://twitter.com/michaelshermer/status/763118324230217728.

mankind the necessity of auxiliary precautions"—mainly involving constitutional government with checks and balances.[33]

Of course, the "Rationalia" of representative and constitutionally limited government hardly guarantees that rational people will run government—our experiences with the 2016 presidential election should prove that beyond any doubt. Yet Shermer can sensibly claim (and I agree) that the general sort of government we have is the best we can rationally hope for (it allows for internal improvements, which we need), and that it gives us the best hope for rational outcomes. As the saying goes, constitutional democracy is terrible, but it is less terrible than other forms of governance.

We should keep in mind that Tyson is talking about a "virtual" country, not a real one. Yet he clearly means his virtual world to be in some respects a model for the real world. It is unclear (to me) whether and to what degree Tyson buys into the rational requirement of representative, constitutionally limited government. Without a means of real-world implementation, Tyson's version of Rationalia remains purely utopian.

If Tyson is saying that a "rational" elite should run society—and his remarks can easily be interpreted that way—then he's obviously and dangerously wrong.

Yet in a deeper sense I take Tyson's side. Some of Tyson's critics essentially argue that people cannot be fully rational, therefore Rationalia (in the real world) won't work. I agree with Tyson that we can be rational, and we can, in fact, build a society on rational principles.

Tyson's problem is that he doesn't know which principles are rational in the realm of politics. His main error is smuggling in false philosophic premises as his standard for what counts as "rational" policy. Thus, my central criticism of Tyson is not that Rationalia is impossible—I think it is possible, in the sense

---

33 *Federalist* #51, https://www.congress.gov/resources/display/content/The+Feder alist+Papers#TheFederalistPapers-51.

outlined by Shermer—it is that Tyson's particular version of Rationalia is fundamentally irrational.

Tyson offers a much more detailed account of his Rationalia in an August 7 Facebook post.[34] Here we can see Tyson's underlying fallacies at work.

I want to walk through Tyson's key remarks and make some first-round criticisms, then step back and draw some broader conclusions.

Tyson says he uses the term "policy" broadly:

> Examples of Policy would be a government's choice to invest in R&D, and if so, by how much. Or whether a government should help the poor, and if so, in what ways. Or how much a municipality should support equal access to education. Or whether or not tariffs should be levied on goods and services from one country or another. Or what tax rate should be established, and on what kinds of income.

Clearly Tyson envisions a powerful government. He does not question whether government should impose taxation— that it should is a given in Tyson's world—he allows room only for debating the nature of taxation. Government "investing" in scientific research is automatically neither in nor out on moral grounds; it depends on the "evidence" about it.

Tyson continues, "In Rationalia, since weight of evidence is built into the Constitution, everyone would be trained from an early age how to obtain and analyze evidence, and how to draw conclusions from it."

Trained . . . by whom? Obviously Tyson has the government in mind. And if a parent does not wish his child to be "trained" by Tyson's educators "from an early age," what then? If Tyson

34   Neil deGrasse Tyson, "Reflections on Rationalia," August 7, 2016, https://www.facebook.com/notes/neil-degrasse-tyson/reflections-on -rationalia/10154399608556613/.

really means "everyone," then he means government should send agents with guns to forcibly remove children from noncompliant parents. I suspect Tyson would walk back some of his remarks if pressed; he doesn't seem to have thought through some of them very carefully.

Next: "In Rationalia, you would have complete freedom to be irrational. You just don't have the freedom to base policy on your ideas if the weight of evidence does not support it."

Obviously Tyson does not really mean "complete freedom"; for example, people wouldn't be free to murder others or (presumably) to engage in female genital mutilation. But what else would Tyson forbid? He's not clear. Would religious parents have "complete freedom" to educate their children as they see fit?

A bit later in his piece, Tyson renegotiates his promise of "complete freedom" for the individual. Instead, he writes, "In Rationalia, research in psychology and neuroscience would establish what level risks we are all willing to take, and how much freedom we might need to forfeit, in exchange for comfort, health, wealth and security." Hello, *1984*.

Note here that Tyson seems to presume that an individual is automatically irrational if he demands freedoms that clash with the risk-aversion, "comfort, health, wealth [or] security" of others. Does Tyson mean a majority? Does he think some utilitarian collective happiness calculation is possible and desirable? He is entirely unclear. Obviously we are not "all" going to agree about appropriate levels of risk, "comfort," and the like—so what is the standard by which the freedom of dissenters will be squashed?

Then there's this: "In Rationalia, you could create an Office of Morality, where moral codes are proposed and debated"—and, presumably, imposed by force. Sort of like what the "rational" Communists did. (The practitioners of totalitarian Islam also have their Offices of Morality, which they'd claim are perfectly rational.)

I'm sure that Tyson does not intend a totalitarian outcome. I am equally sure that a future "scientific" totalitarian could plausibly claim to be in complete compliance with the terms for Rationalia that Tyson lays out.

That Tyson is deeply statist in political orientation is beyond reasonable doubt: He wants a powerful government to substantially control key aspects of each person's life, including each person's wealth, education, and morals. What is the source of this statism?

Undergirding Tyson's statist vision of Rationalia is a philosophic presumption of collectivism, the view that society as a whole is the basic standard of value, and that individuals, their values, and their proclaimed rights may be sacrificed for the sake of society.

Does an individual not wish to subject his children to the government's "training" regimen? Not wish to finance government-approved R&D or "art in schools" or government research into "the sciences that study human behavior" or whatever else the "rational" class might concoct? Not wish to surrender his freedoms for the proclaimed "comfort, health, wealth and [or] security" of others? Not wish to obey the dictates of the Office of Morality? Too bad. The individual, his values, his rights (not that Tyson seems to recognize the existence of rights), his liberties, his wealth, his children, presumably his very life, all may be demanded by the self-proclaimed "rational" rulers.

What is the rational basis of Tyson's collectivism? He offers none. His entire "rational" structure is built on an irrational, unjustified (and unjustifiable) philosophic presumption.

Of course, in the scope of a short article such as this, I cannot justify the moral theory that an individual rightly pursues his own life and values, nor the political theory that individuals have rights. The point here is that, to establish that your politics are rational, you have to actually recognize the moral underpinnings of your politics and, ultimately, show that they, too, are rational. Tyson doesn't even seem to realize that he's presuming unjustified collectivist moral premises.

Some might deem my criticisms of Tyson overly harsh. Isn't Tyson in important ways just arguing for the status quo? Obviously government today confiscates people's wealth, runs schools, finances R&D, prohibits various "immoral" behaviors, and so on—in important ways Tyson follows convention, not reason. Yes, I decry the collectivism at work in today's politics. But at least the (often implicit) collectivism of today is mixed with an (often explicit) individualism, and at least it does not formally bear the mantle of rationality. By claiming to base a society on rationality, and by grounding that society on collectivist premises, Tyson gives collectivism a dangerously broader sanction and potential. Quite simply, collectivism taken to its "rational" conclusions results in totalitarianism, always and necessarily.

I'll pick up the fundamental moral debate another day. Here I will conclude by pointing out that Shermer's version of Rationalia—the Founders' version—is compatible with individualism: The view that each person morally pursues his own values and happiness, consonant with the rights of others. (I don't agree with all of Shermer's particular political conclusions.) The project of American governance is, at its core, based on people's "unalienable Rights," chiefly each person's rights to "Life, Liberty and the pursuit of Happiness."

Tyson includes this gem in his discussion: "In Rationalia, . . . [e]veryone would have a heightened capacity to spot bullshit wherever and whenever it arose." Thankfully, we don't need to live in Tyson's Orwellian version of Rationalia to spot his bullshit collectivist moral premises.

# Sam Harris's Collectivist Politics

SAM HARRIS—NEUROSCIENTIST AND FAMED ATHEIST—holds that matters of right and wrong, good and bad are discoverable, objective facts, properly the subject of a science of ethics. In his 2010 book *The Moral Landscape*, he writes in his introduction, "questions about values—about meaning, morality, and life's larger purpose—are really questions about the well-being of conscious creatures. Values, therefore, translate into facts that can be scientifically understood" (p. 1).[35]

So far, so good. Unfortunately, Harris quickly veers off the scientific track by defining "well-being" in terms of the moral theory of utilitarianism. Utilitarianism holds that the standard of moral value is "the greatest good for the greatest number"; in practice, this means the individual must self-sacrificially serve the interests of society.

Harris explicitly ties his views to the utilitarian tradition of Jeremy Bentham and John Stuart Mill, though he says "[c]onsequentialism has undergone many refinements" since the days of Bentham and Mill (p. 207, n. 12). In this tradition, the standard of moral value is the aggregate happiness of all people.

---

35 All parenthetical citations within this essay refer to Sam Harris, *The Moral Landscape: How Science Can Determine Human Values* (New York: Free Press, 2010).

Although Harris recognizes some of the problems with attempting to aggregate the well-being of everyone, he insists that "human welfare must aggregate in *some* way" (pp. 68, 72).[36] Indeed, the "some way" in which utilitarianism aggregates human welfare is by sacrificing the individual to the alleged greater good of the group. If that sounds ominously similar to the moral foundation of the political nightmares of the 20th century, that's because it is.

Remarkably, Harris is, at times, quite open about the implications of utilitarianism and serious about promoting them, noting that the doctrine can justify the murder of individuals—or large numbers of individuals—for the presumed greater good. For example, Harris writes:

> Admittedly, it is difficult to know how we should treat all of the variables that influence our judgment about ethical norms. If I were asked, for instance, whether I would sanction murder of an innocent person if it would guarantee a cure for cancer, I would find it very difficult to say "yes," despite the obvious consequentialist argument in favor of such an action. If I were asked to impose a one in a billion risk of death on everyone for this purpose, however, I would not hesitate. (p. 143)

Harris goes further, wondering whether "it would be ethical for our species to be sacrificed for the unimaginably vast happiness of some superbeings." He answers: "Provided that we take the time to really imagine the details (which is not easy), I think the answer is clearly 'yes.'" Although Harris notes that "there is no compelling reason to believe that such superbeings exist," he acknowledges that, on his theory, if they did, humans would be morally bound to willingly accept their own annihilation (p. 211, n. 50).

---

36  Harris also argues that in order to act morally humans must take into account the well-being of animals—see, for example, *The Moral Landscape*, p. 63—but that detail is outside the scope of this essay.

At other times, Harris walks back from the logical implications of his theory, opting instead for a watered-down utilitarianism in which individuals succumb to their "selfish" nature and act only to a limited extent for the happiness of all "conscious creatures." In other words, in light of complications that arise from his theory, he recommends cheating on it. And, as an example of appropriate ways to cheat, Harris takes a page from his own life.

Citing such tragedies as the fact that some "people on earth needlessly starve to death," Harris writes of his own frequent inattention to such matters: "I am less good than I could be. Which is to say, I am not living in a way that truly maximizes the well-being of others" (p. 82). How does Harris rationalize acting against his own standard of value? How, for instance, does he justify failing to reduce his own (and his family's) standard of living to near-subsistence so that he can send the residual to the starving people of the world? Essentially, he argues that people (himself included) are too narrowly "selfish" to fully live up to the utilitarian ideal; people are not constituted such that they can act fully morally. As he puts it, "We are not, by nature, impartial— and much of our moral reasoning must be applied to situations in which there is tension between our concern for ourselves, or for those closest to us, and our sense that it would be better to be more committed to helping others" (p. 40). The best we can do, says Harris, is to resolve the conundrum pragmatically: "What we can do is try, within practical limits, to follow a path that seems likely to maximize both our own well-being and the well-being of others. This is what it means to live wisely and ethically" (p. 85).

Harris attempts to persuade readers that acting more in accordance with the utilitarian ideal would make them personally happier, but he cannot persuade even himself of this:

> I know that helping people who are starving is far more important than most of what I do. I also have no doubt that doing what is most important would give me more pleasure and emotional satisfaction. . . . But this knowledge does not change me. I still want to do what

> I do for pleasure more than I want to help the starving
> . . . . I would be happier if I were less selfish. This means
> I would be more wisely and effectively selfish if I were less
> selfish. (p. 83)

Harris recognizes that upholding his utilitarian standard of value—the greatest happiness for the greatest number—is simply impossible. Hence, he condones cheating on it.

To the degree that Harris is true to his collectivist underpinnings, they push him toward totalitarian politics.

Harris acknowledges that "many people are simply wrong about morality" (p. 87). Within an individualist theory of morality, that poses no special problem: So long as people don't aggress against others, they are free to be wrong; and if some people do aggress against others, they are properly prosecuted as criminals. Within Harris's utilitarian framework, however, the fact that many err in their moral thinking and acting creates a moral crisis for everyone. And, as Harris has admitted, no one— including Harris—can uphold the utilitarian ideal of serving the greatest happiness of the greatest number.

If people morally should serve the greater good of the group but do not, can they be left free to be immoral? How will we know whether people's actions are really in the best interest of the group? Who will decide such matters? According to Harris, "moral experts" will decide.

That others have noticed totalitarian implications in Harris's theory prompted him to repeatedly deny such implications. For instance, when Harris wrote that "only genuine moral experts would have a deep understanding of the causes and conditions of human and animal well-being" (p. 36), he added the following in a footnote:

> Many people find the idea of "moral experts" abhorrent. Indeed, this ramification of my argument has been called "positively Orwellian" and a "recipe for fascism." . . . [T]hese concerns seem to arise from an uncanny reluctance to think about what the concept of "well-being" actually

entails or how science might shed light on its causes and conditions. The analogy with health seems important to keep in view: Is there anything "Orwellian" about the scientific consensus on the link between smoking and lung cancer? (p. 202, n. 17)[37]

But this analogy fails. On an individualist conception of morality, nothing in a scientific finding on the physiological effects of smoking implies that the government should ban or restrict smoking (at least not for adults on private property). When people are seen as individuals—with each individual being morally responsible for his own life, health, and happiness—people are free to act as they choose so long as they do not violate the rights of others. If someone chooses to ignore scientific findings or medical experts and proceeds to smoke himself ill, that is his choice and his problem.

On a collectivist moral ideal, however, individuals are not seen as responsible for their own lives, health, and happiness; rather, they are regarded as responsible for everyone's life, health, and happiness. To be moral, according to utilitarianism, people must act so as to achieve the greatest happiness for the greatest number—and they must sacrifice their personal goals and values to achieve that end. This collectivist moral framework necessitates a collectivist political program. If the collective or the "moral experts" decide it is best for the individual to be forbidden from smoking—or forbidden from doing anything else, or required to do anything else—then the individual morally must obey.

Concerns about Harris's call for "moral experts" to determine the best ways for people to live up to the utilitarian ideal are hardly quelled by his additional call for manipulating individuals' brains. Consider Harris's following remarks (in which he leaves "we" undefined):

---

37   See also Sam Harris, "Response to Critics of the Moral Landscape," January 29, 2011, http://www.samharris.org/site/full_text/response-to-critics.

If . . . we can one day manipulate the brain so as to render specific behaviors and states of mind more pleasurable than they are now, it seems relevant to wonder whether such refinements would be "good." It might be good to make compassion more rewarding than sexual lust, but would it be good to make hatred the most pleasurable emotion of all? (p. 196, n. 20; see also pp. 102, 109)

After denying "that the mere existence of the Nazi doctors counts against my thesis," Harris writes:

If we were ever to arrive at a complete understanding of the human mind, we would understand human preferences of all kinds. Indeed, we might even be able to change them. . . . Consider how we would view a situation in which all of us miraculously began to behave so as to maximize our collective well-being. Imagine that on the basis of remarkable breakthroughs in technology, economics, and politic skill, we create a genuine utopia on earth.[38]

Harris writes this as though nothing were troublesome about the notion of "moral experts" and some undefined "we" "manipulating" people's brains to "create a genuine utopia on earth" through "breakthroughs in technology, economics, and politic skill." A skeptic, however, perhaps someone with an "uncanny reluctance" to think about things from Harris's perverse perspective, might respond that the 20th century produced quite enough such "breakthroughs" on the road to utopia. And the utilitarian regimes of that century did not yet have the power of today's or tomorrow's neuroscientists to manipulate people's brains.

---

38  Sam Harris, "Response to Critics of the Moral Landscape," January 29, 2011, http://www.samharris.org/site/full_text/response-to-critics.

But just imagine, Harris continues, if we could alter the brains of everyone by "painlessly deliver[ing] a firmware update to everyone":

> Now the entirety of the species is fit to live in a global civilization that is as safe, and as fun, and as interesting, and as filled with love as it can be. . . . [I]f you care about something that is not compatible with a peak of human flourishing—given the requisite changes in your brain, you would recognize that you were wrong to care about this thing in the first place. Wrong in what sense? Wrong in the sense that you didn't know what you were missing.[39]

How is Harris's proposal here different from the Borg Collective in *Star Trek*? What if an individual does not care to undergo brain surgery to discover what he has been missing? Would the "moral experts" say, as do the Borg, "Resistance is futile?"

Because Harris's moral framework evaluates individuals and their actions by the standard of collective well-being, it is incompatible with the principle of individual rights. Harris appears to acknowledge and accept this: "Some people worry that a commitment to maximizing a society's welfare could lead us to sacrifice the rights and liberties of the few wherever these losses would be offset by the greater gains of the many." Not to worry, he says: "To the degree that treating people as ends in themselves is a good way to safeguard human well-being, it is precisely what we should do" (p. 79).

Of course, "treating people as ends in themselves" only insofar as that serves the collective "good" is not treating people as ends in themselves; it is treating them as means to the ends of the collective. And "to the degree that treating people as ends in themselves" does not serve the collective good—a determination

---

39   Sam Harris, "Response to Critics of the Moral Landscape," January 29, 2011, http://www.samharris.org/site/full_text/response-to-critics.

to be made by the "moral experts"—individuals and their rights must be sacrificed.

So what is the individualist alternative?

Harris is right that morality should be based in reality and viewed as a science discoverable through reason. He is right that morality pertains to well-being, and that ethics prescribes the means to achieving it. But he is wrong in embracing a utilitarian, collectivist standard; wrong in sanctioning the sacrifice of individuals to the collective; wrong in obliterating the principle of individual rights and paving the way for more totalitarianism.

Decades before the publication of Harris's book, Ayn Rand formulated an individualist morality that anticipates everything salvageable in Harris's work and avoids all of its problems.

Unfortunately, at least as of May 2012, Harris refuses to read Rand's works, saying "my copies of [Rand's novels] *The Fountainhead* and *Atlas Shrugged* simply would not open."[40] (Isn't there a "firmware update" for that?) Not surprisingly, in attempting to describe Rand's ethical views he fundamentally misrepresents them.[41]

If Harris would consider the possibility that collectivism is false, he would be closer to finally being able to articulate a viable alternative to the moral relativism and religious dogma he so rightly despises.

---

40  Sam Harris, "How to Lose Readers (Without Even Trying)," August 25, 2011, http://www.samharris.org/blog/item/how-to-lose-readers-without-even-trying.

41  See Ari Armstrong, "Sam Harris Couldn't Help But Smear Ayn Rand," *Objective Standard*, May 17, 2012, http://www.theobjectivestandard.com/blog/index.php/2012/05/sam-harris-couldnt-help-but-smear-ayn-rand.

# "You Didn't Build That" —Obama's Ode to Envy

BARACK OBAMA'S JULY 13, 2012 SPEECH,[42] in which he tells business owners, "you didn't build that," has rightly generated enormous criticism. But why did he say it? Before we turn to that question, let's review exactly what Obama said:

> [I]f you've been successful, you didn't get there on your own. . . . I'm always struck by people who think, well, it must be because I was just so smart. There are a lot of smart people out there. It must be because I worked harder than everybody else. Let me tell you something— there are a whole bunch of hardworking people out there.
>
> If you were successful, somebody along the line gave you some help. There was a great teacher somewhere in your life. Somebody helped to create this unbelievable American system that we have that allowed you to thrive. Somebody invested in roads and bridges. If you've got a business—you didn't build that. Somebody else made

---

that happen. The Internet didn't get invented on its own. Government research created the Internet so that all the companies could make money off the Internet.

The point is, is that when we succeed, we succeed because of our individual initiative, but also because we do things together.

This speech is remarkable only for its ludicrousness. (It is certainly not remarkable for its originality; as others have noted, Obama took a page out of Elizabeth Warren's campaign book.[43] Then again, Obama would say she didn't write that.)

Obama wishes us to believe that the successful—whatever their field and scale of success—are wrong to attribute their success to applying their minds and working hard. Unfortunately for Obama, rational Americans know that his claim contradicts the facts surrounding the achievements of every productive industrialist, producer, and creator, who succeeds by thinking, planning, and working hard.

Examples range from J. D. Rockefeller, who revolutionized the oil industry; to the Wright brothers, who pioneered heavier-than-air human flight; to Thomas Edison, who developed a usable electric light bulb (among other innovations); to Ayn Rand, who wrote great novels on the themes of independence, individual productiveness, and the role of reason in man's life; to Steve Jobs, who revolutionized the computer, music, and film industries.

Obama wishes us to believe that, because not every "smart," hard-working person reaches the pinnacle of success, that somehow diminishes the achievements of those who do. True enough, some "smart" people misapply their intelligence,

---

43  See Lucy Madison, "Elizabeth Warren: 'There Is Nobody in this Country Who Got Rich on His Own,'" CBS News, September 22, 2011, http://www.cbsnews .com/news/elizabeth-warren-there-is-nobody-in-this-country-who-got-rich-on -his-own/; and Ari Armstrong, "Elizabeth Warren's 'Social Contract' an Ideological Fantasy," PJ Media, September 28, 2011, https://pjmedia.com/blog/elizabeth -warrens-social-contract-an-ideological-fantasy/?singlepage=true.

for instance, by becoming animal "rights" activists or Marxist community organizers. Others go into business without having the right business plan, the right motivation, the right leadership skills, or the right good or service for their intended market; indeed, only a third of businesses survive their first decade.[44] Often entrepreneurs fail numerous times before developing a successful business. Rational Americans understand that, while not every smart, hard-working person builds a successful business, that does not alter the fact that those who do build successful businesses do so by thinking, planning, and working hard.

Obama also wishes us to believe that, because successful producers learned something from government teachers, used government roads and bridges, employed government research, and the like, this means they don't really own their success or wealth. Rational Americans know full well that the government funds such things by forcibly confiscating the wealth of producers. Rational Americans also know that a bum is as free to use a government bridge as is a successful business owner, but the business owner chose to apply his intelligence and work hard to build something great.

Finally, to mask the inanity of what he just said, Obama mentions that "individual initiative" perhaps has *something* to do with a producer's success. But, in addition to seeing through Obama's flagrant contradictions, rational Americans see this subordination for exactly what it is: an attempt to insignificantly mitigate what he said before, while leaving what he said before as his main and emphatic message.

Of course, that Obama flouts logic and observable facts is obvious to anyone who spends even a few moments evaluating his claims. Why, then, does he spout such nonsense?

---

44  Scott Shane, "Why Do Most Start Ups Fail?," *Small Business Trends*, September 26, 2011, http://smallbiztrends.com/2011/09/why-do-most-start-ups-fail.html. Estimates of business failure vary, of course.

To understand the atmosphere in which Obama delivered his remarks, watch the video.[45] When Obama tells business leaders, "You didn't get there on your own," some in the crowd chant, "That's right!" When Obama ridicules business leaders for thinking they're "just so smart," many in the crowd meet his comments with jeering laughter.

The purpose of Obama's speech was not to present serious arguments about the causes of success in business. His claims are ridiculous on their face. Obama's purpose was to give envious Americans the pretext they need to openly loathe those who have been successful—and to vote accordingly.

If the successful didn't really earn their success—and thus the wealth that comes with it—then there's nothing wrong with "spreading their wealth around" to those who have not been so successful. If no one is responsible for his success, then no one has a right to the fruits of his success, and thus those who haven't been successful have the same right to those fruits. And if the successful resist the "noble" effort to redistribute what is "really" the community's wealth, then they are evil—or so Obama wishes us to believe.

In reality, anyone who develops a new technology, writes a great novel, brings an innovative new product to market, or in any other way earns success, thereby deserves the fruits of that success. Unfortunately for Obama, rational Americans know this, and rational Americans will win this debate.

---

45   A segment of the talk is posted by GOP Rapid Response at https://www.youtube.com/watch?v=YKjPI6no5ng.

# The Justice of Income
# Inequality Under Capitalism

MANY "OCCUPY WALL STREET" PROTESTERS (active in 2011 and the years following) oppose the bailouts of failed banks and financial institutions. They are right to do so: Such bailouts violate rights by forcibly transferring wealth from some people to others via taxes, deficit spending (future taxes), and monetary expansion (hidden taxes). At the same time, however, many Occupiers call for even more forced wealth transfers for things such as unemployment payments, student loans, mortgage support, government schools, and "green" energy. Why do many Occupiers oppose some forced wealth transfers and advocate others?

The answer may be found in the popular "occupation" phrase: "We are the 99 percent." As *Vanity Fair* explained earlier this year, "The upper 1 percent of Americans are now taking in nearly a quarter of the nation's income every year. In terms of wealth rather than income, the top 1 percent control 40 percent."[46] The 99 percent, then, consist of everyone else. According to the typical Occupier, politicians should forcibly seize wealth, so long

---

46  Joseph E. Stiglitz, "Of the 1%, By the 1%, For the 1%," *Vanity Fair*, March 31, 2011, http://www.vanityfair.com/news/2011/05/top-one-percent-201105.

as they seize it from the relatively wealthy and give it to those with less. "Tax the Rich" (even more), many protest signs read. *Vanity Fair* compares America's wealthy to Middle Eastern theocratic dictators: "Americans have been watching protests against oppressive regimes that concentrate massive wealth in the hands of an elite few." The magazine predicts that "even the wealthy will come to regret" the income inequality in this country. While some in the "Occupy Wall Street" movement may attempt to make good on that threat, if income inequality is their concern, they should instead consider some history.

True, throughout most of human history, great income inequality arose when the political class looted the masses. Slaves labored in Egypt to build elaborate burial pyramids for their jewel-crested Pharaohs. In the socialist Soviet Union, the "dictators of the proletariat" lived lavishly even as they starved millions to death while selling grain to other countries (for details, see the film *The Soviet Story*). Thus, while some Occupiers call to replace capitalism with socialism (see the Denver college professor and "born-again Trotskyite" or the Los Angeles Occupier calling for bloody revolution),[47] if successful their strategies would in fact create another kind of income inequality.

But the income inequality under tyranny is fundamentally different from that under capitalism. One arises from looting and forcing; the other from producing and thinking. Looters seize available wealth. They add nothing to the supply of wealth, opting instead to smash things, divert human effort to the task of looting, and squash the incentive of their victims to produce much of anything. Thus, even if looters could achieve income equality, doing so would constitute a moral atrocity. Producers

---

47   Kelly Maher, "Let's Replace Capitalism," October 13, 2011, https://www .youtube.com/watch?v=hI7JjwTSTfs; "Occupy LA Speaker Calls Gandhi A 'Tumor,' Pushes For Violent 'Revolution,'" CBS Los Angeles, October 12, 2011, http://losangeles.cbslocal.com/2011/10/12/occupy-la-speaker-calls-ghandi-a -tumor-pushes-for-violent-revolution/.

create new wealth: They restructure their own resources—
their land, machinery, seeds, and minerals—to create goods
and services that benefit human life. Producers earn money
by trading voluntarily with those who also benefit from the
exchange. Often producers hire others, improving the lot of
employer and employee alike.

Looters win (in their own short-sighted view) at the expense
of others. Producers win as they help others win. At worst, a
looter takes your life; at best, he steals what you produce. At
worst, a producer leaves you alone; at best—and most typically—
he greatly enriches and expands our lives.

America's capitalists have nothing in common with
dictators in the Middle East or with any other type of looter. (I
mean actual capitalists, not those pretenders in business who
wield political power to seize subsidies and hamstring their
competitors.) Steve Jobs did not earn a fortune by attacking
others or stealing from them; he grew wealthy by building
remarkably advanced machines that dramatically improve
the lives of tens of millions of people. Whatever wealth Jobs
personally gained, he added enormously more value to his
customers' lives. The same can be said of any of America's
business leaders, whether the energy producer George
Mitchell, retailer Jeff Bezos, software developer Bill Gates,
internet visionary Mark Zuckerberg, or anybody else who lives
by thinking and producing at whatever scale. Producers trade
goods and services for money, and the exchange benefits both
parties. A producer's wealth indicates the scope of his mutually
beneficial exchanges.

From the economic point of view, as Ludwig von Mises wrote
in a 1955 letter: "Destitution is in a feudal society the corollary
of income inequality, but not in a capitalist society. The fact that
there is 'big business' does not impair, but improve the conditions

of the rest of the people."[48] Mises writes here of productive business in a free economy, not politically-connected "business" that seeks reward in handouts and special favors. To the degree that today's economy has brought some closer to destitution, the cause is not productive big business, but instead the looting mentality of inflationary government spending, political support for irresponsible mortgages, bailouts for banks and unions, out-of-control entitlements, corporate welfare, and the like. In short, the cause is government interference in the economy.

From the moral point of view, forcibly seizing wealth from producers violates their rights. The relevant moral distinction is not between the 99 percent and the wealthiest one percent, but rather between the producers and the looters on any scale. The great producers of our society do not deserve envious snarls and threats to forcibly seize their property. Instead, they deserve our gratitude and admiration.

---

48  Ludwig von Mises, letter to John Van Sickle dated February 24, 1955. I reviewed this letter (among many others) with the permission of, and in the former Boulder home of, John's son Jerry. Jerry donated the set of letters to the Foundation for Economic Education, which publishes the first page of the 1955 letter at https://fee.org/media/4918/mises-to-van-sickle-p1.pdf.

# Egalitarianism versus Rational Morality on Income Inequality

As CATO'S ALAN REYNOLDS POINTS OUT, various pundits (including Paul Krugman) have, based on the work of Thomas Piketty, declared that the percentage of income and wealth of the top 1 percent has surged in recent years.[49] As Reynolds demonstrates, those pundits are wrong. But Reynolds's analysis will hardly persuade today's egalitarians to alter their policy goals of higher taxes and more regulations, because they regard *any* income inequality as morally suspect if not outright offensive.

Regarding income (i.e., annual earnings), Reynolds points out that comparing prewar and postwar income is tricky due to different standards in calculating income. Whereas Piketty's figures suggest that the top 1 percent of earners collect nearly 20 percent of income, a more realistic comparison (based on tax adjusted "modified personal income") shows that "the Top 1% share clearly spiked upward after the 1986 Tax Reform [from

---

49   Alan Reynolds, "Piketty Problems: Top 1% Shares of Income and Wealth Are Nothing Like 1917–28," Cato Institute, May 20, 2014, http://www.cato.org/blog/piketty-problems-top-1-shares-income-wealth-are-nothing-1917-28.

around 8 percent], and then fluctuated cyclically between 11 and 13 percent from 1988 to 2011, averaging 12.3 percent."

Regarding wealth (i.e., accumulated assets), Reynolds points out that there is no evidence showing the top 1 percent of wealth holders now hold more wealth; indeed, their share of wealth declined from 40 percent in 1930 to 21 percent in 2000. (Of course, different individuals continually join and leave this group.)

To egalitarians, though, Reynolds's figures only serve to demonstrate that inequalities of income and wealth, whatever the details, are dramatic. Whether the top 1 percent of earners bring in 12 percent or 20 percent of total income, egalitarians will point out, that's still a hugely disproportionate amount of wealth. It's not like any egalitarian will read Reynolds's report and say, "Thank God; the top 1 percent earn only 12.3 percent of all income." Instead, egalitarians (if they accept Reynolds's figures) will proclaim, "The fact that the top 1 percent earn 12.3 percent of all income is a moral outrage!" They'd say the same thing if the figure were 5 percent.

To egalitarians, the mere fact that one person earns more income or acquires more wealth than does another person is automatically morally suspicious, regardless of context. To egalitarians, having more wealth than someone else is morally permissible only to the degree that the person guilty of having more wealth continually apologizes for it and self-sacrificially works to eliminate the disparity.

And what is the basis for the egalitarian moral framework? Why is the fact that some people earn more than others do morally wrong? What reasons do egalitarians provide in support of their position that such inequality is wrong? The fantasy world imagined by egalitarian philosopher John Rawls notwithstanding, egalitarians provide no reasons at all.

What, then, is the proper moral framework for assessing the significance of income inequality? The proper framework is a morality based on perceptual observations of the factual requirements of human life.

As Ayn Rand observed, people need to pursue values in order to live. As human beings, we *produce* the values we need to live and prosper by the rational use of our minds—our fundamental means of survival. To live and prosper, an individual needs the freedom to produce values and to trade values with others who produce them so that he can acquire the things he needs to live and prosper. Accordingly, he needs government to protect his rights to produce, to trade, and to act on his judgment, free from the initiation of force by others. A proper morality counsels each individual to rationally pursue his life-serving values and his own happiness—and to respect the rights of others to do the same—and, if he does this, the amount of wealth he produces and acquires relative to others is morally irrelevant.

By the standards of a rational morality, one person's need—or his relative lack of wealth—does not impose on anyone else a moral obligation of any kind, let alone an obligation to self-sacrificially serve that person's needs or to give him wealth. (Obviously, rationally self-interested people may choose to charitably help others about whom they care as a means of upholding their personal values.)

By the standards of a rational morality, someone who earns enormous wealth through productive effort morally deserves that wealth and should be admired for having earned it. By a rational morality, magnificently successful producers such as Steve Jobs, John D. Rockefeller, Bill Gates, and Henry Ford (to name a few) are moral heroes by virtue of having produced such great amounts of wealth in the service of their own lives and happiness. (By contrast, according to a rational morality, someone who obtains wealth through force or fraud is immoral.)

By the standards of egalitarianism, the fact that the top 1 percent earned a larger portion of income following the reduction of top tax rates in the 1980s is cause to morally condemn those who lowered tax rates and those who earned more wealth. By the standards of a rational morality, the fact that people produce more wealth when government seizes less of their wealth is cause for demanding that government seize continually less.

In a free market, a market in which government consistently protects everyone's rights to produce and trade by his own judgment (our government does this only partially), no one is harmed by the fact that some people produce vastly more wealth than others do and therefore earn vastly more income and acquire vastly more wealth. Indeed, in a free market, one person's gain typically is another person's gain—for example, I use the computers and telephones produced by Steve Jobs's company, drive the cars produced by Henry Ford's company, and so on. I'd have no access to such values but for the massive earnings of the people who produced and sold them.

If, in a free market, the top 1 percent earned half or more of all income (as unlikely as that is), that would be wonderful news by rational standards. It would mean that a relative few were making astounding advances in business and technology and producing vastly better or more abundant goods and services, thereby enriching themselves and making available for me and for everyone else more life-serving products to purchase and use.

Egalitarianism demands that wealth producers feel guilty about their wealth and self-sacrificially serve others as penance for having wealth. A rational morality counsels wealth producers to take pride in their productive achievements and to seek ever-higher productive achievements for selfish gain.

Egalitarianism encourages people to express envy toward the most successful producers and to publicly shame them. A rational morality treats producers at whatever level, to the degree that they pursue rationally selfish goals to the best of their ability, as moral heroes deserving admiration and praise.

Egalitarianism promotes a government that shackles the most successful producers and seizes their wealth for unearned distribution to others. A rational morality calls for a government that protects the rights of every individual—rich, poor, and in between—to produce and trade by his own judgment and for his own benefit, and to keep and use his wealth as he sees fit.

Inequality of wealth, although inherently neither good nor bad, is, in a free market, perfectly moral—and it is a corollary of magnificent productive achievements. Egalitarianism, on the other hand (in the sense under discussion here), is evil in its every manifestation and to its very core.

# Challenging the Inequality Narrative

Is THERE SOMETHING IMMORAL ABOUT THE FACT that such great creators and producers as author J. K. Rowling, business leader Steve Jobs, and football star Peyton Manning earned enormous wealth, or should their achievements and resulting wealth be celebrated?

Many leaders in politics and academia offer, at best, a mixed appraisal of those who earn great wealth, claiming (among other things) that their wealth isn't really earned, anyway.

Usually when Barack Obama mentions accumulated wealth it is to question its legitimacy. On March 22, 2016, Obama gave a speech in Cuba, a nation whose people for decades have been subjected by their Communistic rulers to abject poverty and political oppression, largely in the name of economic equality.[50]

In his remarks, Obama conceded that Cuba's leadership recognizes some of the "flaws in the American system," flaws including "economic inequality." Among the "enormous problems in our society," Obama said, is "the inequality that concentrates so much wealth at the top of our society." Unlike Marx and many

---

50   Ryan Teague Beckwith, "Read President Obama's Speech to the Cuban People," *Time*, March 22, 2016, http://time.com/4267933/barack-obama-cuba-speech-transcript-full-text/.

of his followers, who call for violent revolution to strip (or kill) those with "so much wealth," Obama said "workers can organize" democratically to achieve greater economic equality.

Obama made greater economic equality a centerpiece of his presidency, and in 2016 Bernie Sanders and Hillary Clinton made it a centerpiece of their campaigns for the presidency.

Whether we look to political debates or to academic discussions, many people these days take it for granted that inequality of wealth is a bad thing (or at least morally suspect) and that politicians should pass laws to take more wealth from the wealthy or to make it harder for people to earn great wealth in the first place.

Don Watkins and Yaron Brook—the team behind the 2013 book *Free Market Revolution* (discussed later in this volume)—do not take the common inequality narrative for granted. Instead, they challenge the notion that economic inequality in a free society is immoral, tackling the issue in the realms of philosophy, history, economics, and politics. The title of their new book indicates their thesis: *Equal Is Unfair: America's Misguided Fight against Income Inequality.*[51]

In their first chapter ("Who Cares about Inequality?"), Watkins and Brook suggest that income inequality is a red herring. What really matters is not how much more income or wealth some people have than others, but "the opportunity to make a better life for ourselves," regardless of where we start or how high we rise (p. 4).

James Truslow Adams referred to "the American Dream" in a 1931 book, Watkins and Brook tell us; in Adams's words, this was "that dream of a land in which life should be better and richer and fuller for everyone, with opportunity for each according to ability or achievement" (p. 5). So the American Dream, properly

51 Don Watkins and Yaron Brook, *Equal Is Unfair: America's Misguided Fight Against Income Inequality* (New York: St. Martin's Press, 2015). Parenthetical notations in this essay refer to that book.

understood, has nothing to do with achieving results equal to others; rather, it is about each person having the freedom to make the most of his own life.

Central to the authors' case is that, to the degree that people are free to do so, we produce wealth and trade goods and services by consent; we do not seize a fixed amount of stuff from others. Watkins and Brook summarize the typical stance of inequality critics: "There is only so much wealth to go around, and so inequality amounts to proof that someone has gained at someone else's expense." But that view is wrong; "because people are constantly creating more wealth," the mere existence of income inequality gives us no "reason to suspect that someone has been robbed or exploited or is even worse off" (p. 8).

One of the strengths of the book is its historical account of great producers, whose existence demonstrates that (where freedom exists) wealth truly is earned and either makes others better off or leaves them unharmed. Whether reviewing the rise of Apple Computer under Steve Jobs and Steve Wozniak (pp. 87–91), the great shipping enterprise of Cornelius Vanderbilt (pp. 148–149), or the productive work or numerous others, Watkins and Brook make clear that those who produce great wealth deserve their great rewards.

What, then, is all the fuss about income inequality? Critics of income inequality claim that, despite the apparent mutual gains of wealth production, the fact that some people earn much more than others does somehow harm others. How? Supposedly the fact that some people earn vast wealth somehow prevents others from advancing and suppresses general economic progress (pp. 5–6). But, as Watkins and Brook show, such claims are bunk.

Watkins and Brook summarize:

> Some economic inequality critics . . . contend that there comes a point at which inequality *undermines* progress—and, by and large, they believe the United States has reached that point today.

What do they base that conclusion on? There is no theoretical reason why differences in income or wealth should slow human progress. . . . Instead, many inequality critics resort to statistically based empirical evidence that tries to draw correlations between high inequality and low growth and low inequality and high growth. (p. 110)

Watkins and Brook spend considerable effort reviewing and refuting many such empirical claims, showing that the critics of inequality misuse the data, ignore relevant data, or improperly interpret the data. In these sections the book becomes policy-wonkish, but the authors do a good job keeping the discussion lively and engaging for a general audience.

To take just one of many examples of these empirical studies: The authors address "a widely touted report from the International Monetary Fund (IMF), which suggest[s] that in underdeveloped countries, higher levels of inequality are correlated with lower rates of economic growth." Based on this study, one leftist referred to the United States as a "banana republic" (p. 110).

The authors reply:

The question is whether inequality lowers growth, and the mere fact that some low-growth economies also have high inequality doesn't answer that question. After all, these high-inequality, underdeveloped countries are also semi- or full-blown dictatorships, where the rulers use political power to exploit people for their own benefit and the benefit of their cronies. It would be ridiculous to draw conclusions about the merits of an economic inequality that emerges from freedom based on an economic inequality that emerges from theft. (p. 111)

Across the board, Watkins and Brook convincingly answer the inequality critics who invoke statistical studies to try to advance their agenda.

In their fifth chapter ("The War on Opportunity"), Watkins and Brook flesh out their argument that the real problem is not inequality of wealth but political impediments to opportunity. They argue that, although economic mobility remains much stronger in the United States than the critics of inequality typically allege, "opportunity *is* under attack today, and the culprit isn't successful people earning huge paychecks. It is the labyrinth of obstacles the government puts in the way of everyone's success—and virtually all of these obstacles are *endorsed* by the critics of inequality" (p. 123).

From outlawing jobs below a "minimum wage," to forcing entrepreneurs to jump through regulatory hoops to start a business, to monopolizing education and driving innovation from the field, to pushing up college costs through subsidies, to taxing away people's wealth, to punishing producers with arbitrary antitrust laws, to tying up health care in bureaucratic red tape, to imposing a motivation-stifling and dependence-inducing welfare state (to mention some of the main areas discussed), modern American government stifles economic opportunity, Watkins and Brook argue.

Although their treatment of these issues will not persuade hardcore critics of capitalism, their case is sufficiently detailed and strong to at least clarify their concerns and to prompt those open to argument to seriously consider their far-reaching proposals.

In their final chapter prior to the conclusion, ("Understanding the Campaign Against Inequality"), Watkins and Brook delve into the philosophic arguments for forcibly limiting income inequality.

Among other things, they critique the view, developed most forcefully by Thomas Nagel and John Rawls, that a person's success or failure is fundamentally a matter of luck. Even a person's "superior character that enables him to make the effort to cultivate his abilities" is a matter of luck, claims Rawls, for it "depends in large part upon fortunate family and social circumstances for which he can claim no credit" (p. 192).

Watkins and Brook respond to such claims:

> Something is clearly wrong here. No honest person believes that Woz [Steve Wozniak] didn't earn the millions he

made at Apple by pioneering the first personal computer, but instead just "got lucky" and "won the lottery." The key error in this argument is that it totally mischaracterizes what it means to earn something. For the egalitarians, the results of our actions don't merely have to be *under our control*, but *entirely of our own making*. (p. 193)

Citing Diana (Brickell) Hsieh's book, *Moral Luck* (discussed later in this volume), Watkins and Brook continue, "In reality, responsibility doesn't require omniscience or omnipotence. It requires only that our actions be voluntary and that we know what we are doing."

Their remark about the meaning of the term "earn" is particularly apt: "We need the concept of 'earn,' not to distinguish people who earn their brains and parents and those who don't, but to distinguish those who use their abilities and resources to create something from those who don't" (pp. 193–194).

Ultimately, Watkins and Brook demonstrate, the egalitarian movement is not about defending the poor, achieving fairness, advancing economic progress, or any such positive goal; rather, it is about stoking envy, encouraging the victim mentality, and demeaning and punishing success. They show this from the realm of philosophy, where some theorists enthusiastically say egalitarianism allows people to "exploit [others] for the common good" (p. 204), to the realm of popular culture, where some people talk about pulling other crabs back into the pot (p. 74), "chopping down the tall poppies" (p. 213), or getting "that bastard" who has wealth (p. 210).

Of course, I have highlighted only a few of the many important elements of the book. Overall, Watkins and Brook have written a profoundly important book at just the right moment in history. If many people read and seriously contemplate this book, it can help save the nation from the morally and economically destructive agenda of the egalitarians.

I do think more work needs to be done, whether by this duo or by others, on the academic arguments for egalitarianism.

Although Watkins and Brook adequately (if briefly) address Rawls's arguments about luck, they don't rebut his claims about the proper conditions for generating social policy (his famous "veil of ignorance"). Nor do they make much headway countering the claims that people with great wealth unduly influence the political system and threaten to undermine representative government. But we shouldn't obsess about what the book doesn't do when it does so much so well.

A personal note: My son as of late 2016 is just over a year old. What will the future look like when he is twenty, thirty, sixty? Will his future be his to make of it what he can—or will his achievements be denied to him or taken away from him for the sake of envy masquerading as a moral theory?

I urge you, to help preserve the American Dream, this Land of Opportunity, to buy this book, read it, and share it. The future can be yours to achieve—if you fight for it.

# An Aristotelian Account
# of Responsibility and Luck

IMAGINE PEOPLE IN THREE DIFFERENT SCENARIOS:

1. Abe and Bill both get blinding drunk at a bar, leave at the same time, and drive home at the same rate of speed. Both run a (different) red light at the same time on the way home. By bad luck, a single mother with her two children is driving through the intersection along Abe's course, and Abe rams his car into hers, killing her and her two children. Bill, on the other hand, makes it home without injuring anyone.

2. Alan and Betty walk along different piers at the same lake. Both are equally brave, but Betty sees a drowning boy in the lake and dives in and saves him. Alan does not see anyone in distress.

3. Adriana and Benjamin are born in very different circumstances. Adriana's parents are wealthy, and she grows up with a good education and many opportunities to improve herself. She becomes a successful neurosurgeon. Benjamin's parents neglect and abuse him and teach him how to steal for them. He becomes an armed robber who winds up in prison.

Why do we blame or praise one individual in each scenario more, given that so much of what they do and what they accomplish depends on luck? Why do we send Abe to prison and sing Betty's praises, but not do the same for their counterparts? Such issues are the subject of Diana (Brickell) Hsieh's book, *Responsibility & Luck: A Defense of Praise and Blame.*[52]

As Hsieh makes clear, one's answers to questions about moral responsibility radically affect one's approach to moral judgment, to criminal justice, and to political policy.

Decisions made in the criminal justice system depend substantially on moral judgments. Hsieh opens her book with the example of a Colorado man who, in 2005, while driving drunk at speeds exceeding one hundred miles per hour, struck and killed another driver. The judge, noting that the man had previously injured someone else while driving drunk and that he had dropped out of an alcohol rehabilitation program, sentenced him "to the maximum penalty of twelve years in prison." Hsieh points out, "According to ordinary moral and legal standards of culpability, [the man] deserved to be blamed and punished for his reckless driving" (p. 1). Yet, according to certain theories with which Hsieh contends in her book, the man was instead himself "a victim of bad luck" (p. 2).

Moral judgments also play a key role in public policy. To draw on an earlier example, if a neurosurgeon is not fundamentally responsible for her success, then how can she deserve her large income? Why should she not be taxed in order to subsidize someone working in fast food? Indeed, if no one deserves his financial successes or failures—if such success or failure is fundamentally a matter of luck (in Barack Obama's terms, "you didn't build that")—then it would seem that the best system is "an egalitarian political order" (p. 9).

In discussing the relationship of moral judgments to politics, Hsieh relates the ideas of Thomas Nagel, who forcefully developed the theory of "moral luck" beginning in 1979, to those of John

---

52 Diana (Brickell) Hsieh, *Responsibility & Luck: A Defense of Praise and Blame* (Sedalia, CO: Philosophy in Action, 2013). Parenthetical notations in this essay refer to that book.

Rawls, whose 1971 *A Theory of Justice* drives today's egalitarian left. Summarizing Nagel's views, she writes:

> [L]uck, in Nagel's sense, influences every action, outcome, or trait for which a person might be judged. An action is shaped by luck even if deliberately chosen because the alternatives open to the person were influenced, if not determined, by circumstances beyond his control. An outcome is shaped by luck even if it unfolds as planned because some chance intervention might have produced a different outcome. Even if cultivated purposefully, character is shaped by luck because a person's most basic moral development might have been radically different if he were born into a different family or culture. So the problem of moral luck represents a sweeping challenge to the practice of moral praise and blame. (p. 7)

This conception of moral luck is also at the base of Rawls's views. As Hsieh explains:

> The problem of moral luck does not merely cast serious doubt on the justice of ordinary moral judgments of persons. By its method of undermining claims of desert, moral luck also offers crucial foundational support for an egalitarian political order. That should be of grave concern to anyone interested in individual liberty and rights.
>
> In *A Theory of Justice*, John Rawls famously argues for egalitarianism as a basic moral principle of social organization on the grounds that people do not earn the favorable or unfavorable circumstances of their birth, including their natural talents. (p. 9)

Hsieh's book is extremely ambitious. It sets out not only to confirm the legitimacy of our "ordinary" moral judgments, but to offer a rich account of the philosophic fundamentals behind those judgments; to affirm the normal, desert-based judgments of the justice system; to elucidate the philosophic bases of criminal and civil law; and to show that, contra egalitarianism, people deserve what they earn.

In developing a positive theory of moral responsibility, Hsieh turns to Aristotle, finding that he solved most of the problems of moral luck long ago. "The heart of his theory consists of his control and epistemic conditions for voluntary action; they identify when a person can be justly praised or blamed on any grounds, moral or otherwise" (p. 69). The control condition means (in brief) that "the person is the source of his actions" (p. 70); he is not driven by outside forces or mental incapacity (such as might be caused by a brain tumor). The epistemic condition means that "a person must act with adequate knowledge of the nature of his actions to be morally responsible for them" (p. 79). An important aspect of the epistemic condition is that a person can be willfully blinded—as by losing his judgment by choosing to get drunk—and still properly be judged for his actions and their outcomes. Although Hsieh discusses many other aspects and details of Aristotle's position—illustrating them with many fascinating examples—the essential theory comes down to this: A person is responsible for his actions if he took them voluntarily and knowingly.

But what of the thorny examples that Nagel raises that seemingly cast doubt on moral judgments as such? Hsieh's main line of counterattack consists of showing that Nagel maintains an unrealistic standard of control: "Nagel implicitly upholds Kant's ideal of 'noumenal agency' by requiring the morally responsible person to exert the all-encompassing power of 'total control'" (p. 45). In other words, Nagel presumes that, to be morally responsible, a person must control every aspect of his moral development, the circumstances of his actions, and the outcomes of his actions. Clearly, such a standard has nothing to do with the real world. For example, although it is true that a drunk driver cannot control other drivers' course and timing, he certainly can control his drinking and his own driving. Thus, if a drunk driver causes a fatal wreck, he is responsible for the consequences—even though those consequences are partly the result of luck.

Hsieh also explains that Nagel ignores the differences between types of moral judgments: "Nagel's arguments for moral luck conflate the distinctive nature and purpose of moral judgments of actions, outcomes, and character. . . . That is unreasonable. These different kinds of moral judgment capture different aspects of a person's moral nature" (p. 189). For example, we can judge the character of a drunk driver and the fact that he drove drunk independently of the consequences of his actions. A drunk driver who causes a fatal crash is properly judged for those consequences, even if another drunk driver luckily did not cause a fatal crash.

Hsieh's ninth chapter, "Responsibility for Character," is perhaps her most useful one for the lay reader. In it, she points out that, although different people face vastly different circumstances in life, each mature individual is fundamentally responsible for the development (or lack thereof) of his moral character. Hsieh explains how a person can mold his moral habits, his moral psychology, and other aspects of his character over time.

These aspects of Hsieh's presentation—and many more not detailed here—add up to an overwhelming case against Nagel's brand of moral luck (and, by extension, against Rawls's brand of egalitarianism). They also offer valuable ideas for judging and therefore interacting with others and for developing one's own moral character.

Although the book is readily accessible to a lay audience, at times it is repetitive, and sometimes its level of technical detail may make for slow and difficult reading. But the material is worth the effort.

In her preface, Hsieh writes, "I'm deeply proud of the results of my efforts. I didn't just solve Thomas Nagel's puzzling 'problem of moral luck,' I developed a rational and robust account of the nature and limits of moral responsibility." Her pride is warranted. But, as Hsieh would insist, each reader of the book should judge for himself.

# A Parable for Thomas Piketty

As complex and difficult as economics can be, I'm always looking for ways to grasp and integrate the principles of the science in simplified and memorable terms. Toward that end, while reading Richard Salsman's clarifying analysis for the *Objective Standard* of Thomas Piketty's *Capital*,[53] I began thinking about Piketty's central argument in terms of a parable. I present the parable below, and I hope it helps you to further integrate the concrete meaning of Piketty's claims and why they are wrong.

My parable was also substantially inspired by Peter and Andrew Schiff's illustrative book *How an Economy Grows and Why It Crashes*.[54] Whereas mine parallels theirs in that it is a story of a man in a fishing community who builds the first fishing net, it differs from theirs in details, and it is nowhere near as elaborate.

Before reading "The Parable of the Fish Capitalist," it will be helpful to read (or review) Piketty's own summary of his central claim:

---

53 Richard M. Salsman, "Piketty's Rickety Assault on Capital," *Objective Standard*, Spring 2015, vol. 10, no. 1, https://www.theobjectivestandard.com/issues/2015-spring/pikettys-rickety-assault-on-capital/.

54 Peter D. Schiff and Andrew J. Schiff, *How an Economy Grows and Why It Crashes* (Hoboken, NJ: John Wiley & Sons, 2010).

[A] market economy based on private property, if left to itself, . . . contains powerful forces of divergence [increasing inequality], which are potentially threatening to democratic societies and to the values of social justice on which they are based. The principle destabilizing force has to do with the fact that the private rate of return on capital, $r$, can be significantly higher for long periods of time than the rate of growth of income and output, $g$. The inequality $r > g$ implies that wealth accumulated in the past grows more rapidly than output and wages. This inequality expresses a fundamental logical contradiction. The entrepreneur inevitably tends to become a rentier [bond holder], more and more dominant over those who own nothing but their labor. Once constituted, capital reproduces itself faster than output increases. The past devours the future. The consequences for the long-term dynamics of the wealth distribution are potentially terrifying. . . . [I]f we are to regain control of capitalism, we must bet everything on democracy . . . [and] develop new forms of governance and shared ownership intermediate between public and private ownership.[55]

As Salsman shows in great technical detail in his review essay of *Capital*, it is not true that the "inequality $r > g$"—even where and when it holds—necessarily leads to ever-increasing inequality, or ever-"reproducing" capital, or the future somehow being "devoured" by the past. Instead, in a market economy, such inequality generally leads to ever-increasing prosperity. Why? Consider the story of Grock.

---

55  Thomas Piketty, *Capital in the Twenty-First Century* (Cambridge, MA: Harvard University Press, 2014), translated by Arthur Goldhammer, pp. 571–73.

## The Parable of the Fish Capitalist

Once upon a time, on a small island in the middle of a vast ocean, toiled a primitive society of one hundred people who ate only fish. Each person was able, using only his hands, to catch a single fish each day, and each fish provided the catcher with enough nutrition for roughly a day.

Because everyone's wealth or lack thereof was essentially equal, this was a society of perfect economic equality. Everyone earned the exact same income—one fish per day—and everyone was equally and horrifically poor. The island people went naked or wore garments hastily woven from leaves. They lived in caves, under bushes, or in shabby lean-tos. They did their best to fend off attacking animals, and occasional pirates, with sticks and rocks. They had no technology aside from simple, handmade tools; no transportation except walking and swimming; no entertainment except singing around the campfire or playing rock-toss games or the like; no health care except the local witch doctor's potions and prayers. But for the lack of fast-food restaurants, tents made from petroleum products, mobile devices, Internet service, nearby emergency clinics, and bongs, the island was an Occupy Wall Streeter's dream come true.

In Piketty's terms, the private rate of return on capital in this island society, $r$, was zero—because there was no capital income and almost zero capital—and the rate of economic growth, $g$, was likewise zero. It was a society in blissful leftist perfection where $r = g$, and no one had to worry about the "terrifying" consequences of expanding capital or inequality. Of course, people frequently died from complications in childbirth, infectious diseases, accidental injuries, animal attacks, and countless other normal circumstances and conditions of primitive society. And, consequently, the average life span was thirty years. But never mind that, for this society avoided the "destabilizing" condition in which $r > g$.

Now one innovative fellow, Grock, got to thinking about a new way to catch fish, and, over the course of much mental effort, he developed an idea for a contraption akin to what we have come to call a net. Inspired by his idea, Grock committed himself to spending some of his rest time working on a physical version of the net. Once in a while he even skipped fishing for a day and went hungry to work on the project. He had no certainty that all this time, effort, and hunger would amount to anything useful, but he took a risk to see his vision through.

When the net was completed, the project had taken Grock a total of eighty hours of work—the equivalent of ten workdays, or the time equivalent of ten hand-caught fish. Excited, but with some trepidation, Grock waded with the net into the cool waters one morning, and . . . joyous day!—by sundown he managed to catch *two* fish, a feat he soon would learn that he could repeat every day. That night, Grock jubilantly celebrated his invention— the first piece of substantial *capital* on the island.

Importantly, Grock did not do anything to harm anyone in the process of creating or using the net, nor did anyone help him in the process of producing it. Of course, he incurred considerable pain and expense himself to make it, and he did so with no guarantee that it would work. But the effort was all his. He alone designed and wove the net. Grock was a sole proprietor, and he was perfectly peaceful.

But Grock's neighbor, Pike, became gravely concerned about Grock's innovation. Pike confronted Grock the morning after Grock's first day of catching two fish.

"Think of the terrifying consequences of your fish net," Pike warned. "Prior to your creation of that device, we lived in blissful utopia in which $r = g$, but now $r > g$! Before, both $r$ and $g$ were zero, but now the capital stock—your net—is worth ten fish, and, given that you now catch an extra fish per day, the private rate of return on capital is one fish daily. But total daily output has not grown by the same percentage; instead, it has grown by only one percent on the first day, from one hundred to one hundred one fish (ninety nine the rest of us catch plus your two). And every day hereafter (with existing capital), $g$ returns to zero. Not only is $r > g$; $r$ is much greater than $g$! Just think where this could lead: Capital could reproduce itself until the past devours the future!"

Grock started to reply, but Pike continued, raising his voice in a mocking tone: "You're probably thinking of your extra fish, and that you're just so smart, and that you worked harder than others to earn your keep. But let me tell you something: There are a lot of smart and hardworking people out there—and they have a hand in your accomplishment. If you were successful in building your net, somebody along the line gave you some help. There was a great teller of tales in your life. Somebody helped beat the path to the waters. If you've got a net—you didn't build that! Somebody else made that happen."[56]

Grock again tried to reply, but Pike continued at even greater volume: "Plus, now your income is twice as much as mine, and that kind of pisses me off. I think maybe we island folk need to exercise some democratic control over your net and develop new forms of shared ownership intermediate between public and private ownership. I think I'll call a meeting to discuss how to handle this."

Pike drew another breath, but this time Grock quickly spoke up: "First, Pike, it is my net, I did build that, I own it, and I'm not going to let you pretend that your 'democratic governance' is anything other than a mob seeking to steal my property.

"Second, Pike, your economics is off. The fact that I now earn a return on my capital investment (i.e., I now get an extra fish per day by using my net) does not by itself imply that my capital stock will continue to grow. Indeed, once in a while I'll have to spend a day mending my net just to keep it in working order. And every once in a while, I'll have to replace it altogether, as the hemp will eventually rot. If I do nothing but that, and if no one else produces any capital, then the total capital stock will remain exactly what it is today.

---

56 This part of Pike's tirade is closely based on Barack Obama's 2012 comments; see Ari Armstrong, "'You Didn't Build That'—Obama's Ode to Envy," *Objective Standard*, July 20, 2012, https://www.theobjectivestandard.com/2012/07/you -didnt-build-that-obamas-ode-to-envy/ (reproduced in this volume).

"Of course, it is true that, now that I have my net, I can devote more of my time to developing other forms of capital—I have a fish farm in mind—and I can offer to pay people more than one fish per day to work for me some days. I think the other island people might appreciate the opportunity to improve their lot in life. They might like some better clothes—maybe even some coverings for their feet—better paths, better places to live, better weapons to fight off animals and pirates, better medicines. Now that I've produced some capital, some of us can spend some of our time working on productive projects other than fishing. That's not terrifying, Pike; it's liberating. With this first piece of capital, we now have the opportunity to expand production and improve the standard of living, not only for ourselves and our children, but also for generations to come.

"Let me point out something that should be obvious, Pike: There's nothing stopping you from building your own net, especially now that you've seen how a net works.[57] If you and everyone else put in the same kind of effort I did to build a net, then the total capital stock would go up a hundred fold (from ten to a thousand), and daily capital income would go up a hundred fold as well (from one to a hundred). But this would not lead to more inequality (not that the degree of inequality is even relevant, so long as no one is stealing other people's stuff). Instead, all else being equal, it would result in everyone earning the exact same amount, two fish per day. The fact is that the relationship of $r$ and $g$, by itself, has nothing to do with the degree of inequality. Everyone can be a capitalist; all that is required is to produce or purchase (invest in) capital. And so long as force and fraud are

---

57  As some critics might point out, a legal system that recognizes patents might indeed prevent others from duplicating and selling a given invention. I do not wish to get into the complexities of the debate over intellectual property here. I will point out that, in a more complex setting, one person's invention, even if patented, does not stop others from producing capital in a practically unlimited number of other ways.

outlawed, everyone can make his own decisions about how he will spend his time.

"Now, it is true that there's no reason to expect that everyone in such a system will be equally successful. Some likely will work harder than others, some will focus on producing capital whereas others will focus on telling stories or some other less-remunerative occupation, some will start with nothing and build great businesses, others will start with great inheritances and slowly squander them, some will make good investments, others will make poor investments. Therefore, we should expect substantial inequality of wealth, and we should welcome it. Inequality in a free society is a consequence of people's natural differences and their freely chosen values, efforts, and actions.

"There is one critical sense in which I want equality, and you apparently do not. I want everyone's rights to be equally protected under the law, such that what a person produces he may keep and do with as he sees fit, and no one else may take it from him by force. You want to destroy equality under the law and replace it with mob rule.

"If everyone's rights are equally protected under the law, it does not matter, morally speaking, that we do not earn or possess equal wealth. What matters is that everyone is free to live and produce and prosper in accordance with his own choices, efforts, and actions.

"Insofar as people's rights are *not* equally protected under the law, certain unjust inequalities (or equalities) of wealth will result. For example, if 'the people' forced some people on the island to give others a fish each week, those others would have substantially more fish than others would. Their "income" would be unequal. The fundamental problem in that case would be the fact that they got the extra fish by means of theft. And the fact that they receive more fish than others would be a derivative aspect of a deeper injustice—the fact that other individuals' property rights were violated. Yes, unequal wealth resulting from theft is immoral. But unequal wealth arising from rights-respecting production is perfectly moral. Production is moral; looting is immoral.

"So, please, let's not hear any more nonsense about how wealth generated by the formation of capital is somehow terrifying, or about how the past will somehow devour the future by people continually improving their standard of living, or about how you want to steal my stuff in the name of democracy."

Pike looked blankly at Grock and said, "I'm sorry, did you say something?" He then proceeded to call for a meeting of the islanders to discuss the pressing problems of Grok's net and of $r$ being greater than $g$.

# Contra Occupiers,
# Profits Embody Justice

ACCORDING TO VARIOUS OCCUPY WALL STREET PROTESTERS, profits hurt people and constitute injustice. For example, an Orange County protester held a sign reading, "People Before Profits"; he told Alex Epstein of the Center for Industrial Progress, "I think people's interests [should] always come first."[58] I interviewed a Zuccotti Park Occupier who said, "In terms of what I'm trying to accomplish and what I would want is a society that actually prioritizes human rights and the notion of social justice over profit."[59]

While such sentiments paint profit as the enemy of rights, justice, and people's well-being, in fact profit in a capitalist system embodies all those things. Set aside for a moment so-called "social justice"—far from undermining justice, protecting the right to profit in a free society is an instance of justice.

---

58  "'Profits Before People?' Alex Epstein visits Occupy Orange County," Center for Industrial Progress, November 20, 2011, https://www.youtube.com/watch?v=7Z2c-Va-hto.

59  Ari Armstrong, "Occupier Calls for More Government Services," November 10, 2011, https://www.youtube.com/watch?v=1A_k_OHHESQ.

What is profit? In the broadest sense, a profit is a gain that comes from exerting personal effort or interacting with others. ("Profit" derives from the Latin term meaning "to make progress.") If I plant tomato seeds and tend the ground, I profit by harvesting the tomatoes. A massage therapist profits by selling that service. Apple profits by trading computers and iPhones (and the services that come with them) for money.

In a free society, people interact by mutual consent, and thus all parties involved in a transaction typically expect to profit. A massage therapist profits by gaining the money, while I profit by gaining the massage. Apple's consumers profit by acquiring the company's devices; the company profits by being paid for them.

The profits of any free, non-fraudulent exchange are necessarily just. Consenting adults have the right to interact voluntarily with others, and each rationally seeks to gain in any exchange of goods or services. This right is part and parcel of the rights to life, liberty, and the pursuit of happiness. (Sometimes people mistakenly anticipate a profit where none is forthcoming, but they have the right to pursue the possibility of profit.) Justice means giving others their due. In a free exchange, each person gets his due—as judged by his own mind on the terms he deems acceptable. A just society recognizes and protects each individual's right to engage in such free exchanges, including lawful contracts that enable complex long-term trades, such as business contracts, sales agreements, insurance policies, and pension plans.

When some parties forcibly interfere with others' right to voluntary exchange and thereby to profit, this is an act of injustice. If the government outlaws massage therapy, or bans terms of compensation agreeable to both parties, or prevents a computer company from charging what it sees fit for its product, or prevents a willing customer from buying it at that price—this unjustly prevents the parties from profiting by mutual agreement.

Nor can one justly profit by means of violating rights. A slaveholder "profits" only by chaining others to a job; the proper term for such a short-sighted gain is not profit but loot. An unscrupulous car salesman loots his customers by lying about the state of the car, thereby committing fraud and taking a customer's money against his consent. A bank robber loots the bank and its customers, stealing their profits. In such cases the government properly intervenes in order to protect people's rights and uphold justice.

Occupy Wall Street is right to complain about the bailouts of politically connected businesses. Such bailouts loot taxpayers and are therefore unjust.

Unfortunately, many Occupy Wall Street protesters call for "social justice," which is a euphemism for more looting. True justice neither needs nor permits the adjective "social" before it. Justice necessarily applies in a social context (the need for justice never arises for a lone individual on a desert island). While justice applies differently in different circumstances, the principle means the same fundamental thing in each: individuals getting what they deserve. Occupiers calling for "social justice" are calling for the use of force to interfere with the voluntary associations of business owners, customers, and employees—for example, through wage and price controls, nullification of loan contracts (e.g., mortgage and education), increased taxes on the so-called one percent, and other forced wealth transfers. "Social justice" is plain injustice.

Profits are good for people, which is why all rational people seek them. Justice is good for people, too, as it enables them to seek profits and forbids people and the government from getting in their way. If Occupiers care about people, they should change their mantra to "Profits and justice for everyone." Or simply: "Capitalism."

# Sparking a Free Market Revolution

STOP LETTING THE ENEMIES OF CAPITALISM claim the moral high ground. There is nothing noble about altruism [i.e., self-sacrifice], nothing inspiring about the initiation of force, nothing moral about Big Government, nothing compassionate about sacrificing the individual to the collective. Don't be afraid to dismiss those ideas as vicious, unjust attacks on the pursuit of happiness, and self-confidently assert that there is no value higher than the individual's pursuit of his own well-being. (p. 220)[60]

So write Yaron Brook and Don Watkins in *Free Market Revolution*, a rallying cry for the morality of capitalism and the self-interested pursuit of profit.

The book is ambitious: In 221 pages of text (excluding front and back matter), the authors seek to explain the nature of capitalism, to define and defend its moral foundation of self-interest, to describe how it has suffered decades of assaults not only from "Progressive" leftists but from altruistic conservatives,

---

60 Yaron Brook and Don Watkins, *Free Market Revolution: How Ayn Rand's Ideas Can End Big Government* (New York: Palgrave MacMillan, 2012). Parenthetical notations in this essay refer to that book.

and to sketch a road map for instituting genuine, laissez- faire capitalism in America.

Part I devotes four chapters to describing "The Problem," beginning with how governmental powers have continually expanded over the past century and a quarter. Drawing on language formulated by their former colleague at the Ayn Rand Institute, Alex Epstein (now the director of the Center for Industrial Progress), the authors next discuss "the argument from greed and the argument from need," the two major claims made for expansive government. Part I closes with a chapter on the housing meltdown, illustrating the points of previous chapters.

Part II, "The Solution," defends rational self-interest and the profit motive, reviews the basic economic case for free markets, recounts the injustices and harms of the regulatory state and the "entitlement" state, and illustrates these points in a chapter devoted to the ailing health-care system. The final chapter explains why "a mixed morality leads inexorably to demands for a mixed economy" (p. 215)—and argues for a consistent morality of rational self-interest and a consistent politics of capitalism.

Although the authors leave unmentioned several important questions that one might expect to see addressed in such a book, they succeed spectacularly in addressing the issues they do field. The book, divided into fourteen short (six to twenty-three page) easy-to-digest chapters, is a joy to read. Even as it merges hefty philosophical arguments, detailed discussions of key economic concepts, and numerous historical examples, its light and breezy prose enables quick reading.

Many of the book's formulations are gems. Consider this: "Business is not a feudal manor but a fellowship of traders" (p. 98). Or this: "[T]he most important way the division of labor makes us more productive is by enabling us to leverage human intelligence" (p. 139). Or this: "The entitlement state is not a safety net but a spiderweb that ensnares and strangles rational, productive, creative, ambitious individuals in order to dole out unearned rewards to the irrational and unproductive" (p. 192).

*Free Market Revolution* is especially powerful in making the following points:

- The "argument from greed" presumes that profit-seeking businessmen are evil and that they therefore must be restrained by the regulatory state.

- The "argument from need" presumes that one person's need imposes a claim on the productive output of others, giving rise to an alleged "right" to health care, education, retirement funds, and the like.

- The basis of both the argument from greed and the argument from need is altruism: the moral code of self-sacrifice. Altruism presumes that self-interested profit seeking is inherently evil and, therefore, that profit seekers must be muzzled and wealth producers looted.

- In the context of a free market, actual selfishness—rational selfishness—consists not of Bernie Madoff-style exploitation of others but of "mutually beneficial production and trade" (p. 67) and the attendant virtues of honesty and integrity, among others.

- "Capitalism is, at its core, the economic system based on the individual's right to seek his own happiness" (p. 42).

In general, the book is written extremely clearly. The only unclear paragraph that stood out to me asserts that the "profit seeker" spurns "*unearned* money" (p. 77). This section fails to distinguish between legitimate gifts and winnings, such as an inheritance or a prize drawing; and illegitimate gains, such as those "mooched from overly generous relatives" (p. 77).

*Free Market Revolution* also leaves unaddressed some important lines of anticapitalist argument. For instance, although the book forcefully argues for private property and against regulations, it does not address concerns about so-called "public goods"—roads, schools, parks, and the like—and why these would be plentiful and largely well-managed when fully and exclusively private. The authors mention in passing that laissez-faire capitalism requires the privatization of roads (p. 217), but they do not address the concerns that commonly accompany this idea. Given its ambitious scope and relative brevity, however, the book may be forgiven such shortcomings.

*Free Market Revolution* could not have come at a better time (appearing in 2012). Given America's continued economic troubles and ballooning debt, Barack Obama's continuous calls for "spreading the wealth around" and controlling businesses, and Paul Ryan's injection of Ayn Rand's ideas into popular discourse (however much Ryan strays from those ideas), Americans are both desperately in need of a principled defense of capitalism and, in many cases, eager to hear it.

*Free Market Revolution* is well worth buying and reading— and more, it is worth promoting among activists, business leaders, students, and anyone concerned with freedom and open to reason.

# The Fruits of Capitalism
# Are All Around Us

THESE ARE SHOCKING STATISTICS: Among Americans ages 18–29, people tend to have a negative view of capitalism and a positive view of socialism.

As Pew reported in 2011, people in this age group saw capitalism negatively by a margin of 47 to 46 percent, and they saw socialism positively by a margin of 49 to 43 percent.[61] This is despite the fact that, to the degree governments have allowed it to exist, capitalism has brought the people of the civilized world vastly more wealth and vastly better and longer life—and despite the fact that socialist governments have slaughtered scores of millions of people.

Overall, people saw capitalism positively only by a margin of 50 to 40 percent. Why does the greatest force for human advancement in the history of the world get such mixed marks among its beneficiaries?

---

61 "Little Change in Public's Response to 'Capitalism,' 'Socialism,'" Pew Research Center, December 28, 2011, http://www.people-press.org/2011/12/28/little -change-in-publics-response-to-capitalism-socialism/.

Today many people confuse capitalism with the cronyism of bank bailouts, corporate welfare, and special government privileges forcibly limiting competition. But such schemes are utterly contrary to capitalism, and it is illogical and unjust to blame capitalism for programs it explicitly opposes. Capitalism is the political-economic system of individual rights and free markets. Under capitalism, government protects individuals' rights to control their own property and interact with others voluntarily. Capitalism forbids fraud, theft, government bailouts, and force of every kind.

When people think of capitalism, they should not think of bank bailouts or the like; rather, they should think of the relatively free aspects of our society and markets, such as freedom of speech, freedom of association, and the relative freedom of the computer industry that has brought us such wonders as remarkably inexpensive yet high-quality laptops, Androids, and iPhones.

Another illustrative example is the modern grocery store. Although the government interferes with the operation of such stores in myriad ways ranging from wage controls to taxation to antitrust actions to food subsidies, in large part grocery stores operate freely, in accordance with the best judgment of their owners and managers. The result is that anyone in the civilized world can quickly and easily purchase goods—including myriad varieties of fresh produce—imported from around the world.

My grandmother, who early in life did not have electricity or even indoor plumbing, spoke of getting an orange for Christmas, and of that being such a delightful treat. Fresh oranges were so rare in those days that they were once-a-year splurges for many families. Today most people take for granted our ability to purchase once-exotic foods from around the world as well as from nearby farms—not only oranges but kiwis, pineapples, pomegranates, coffee and tea in endless varieties, leafy greens, various grains and seeds including quinoa and buckwheat, many types of peppers, many types of meats, various cheeses, and on and on.

The American grocery store even helped bring down Soviet Communism, as Chris Anderson relates in his book *The Long*

*Tail.* While visiting the United States, some 50,000 Soviet citizens witnessed, firsthand, American abundance. After visiting a Houston supermarket, Boris Yeltsin, the first president of post-Soviet Russia, said:

> When I saw those shelves crammed with hundreds, thousands of cans, cartons, and goods of every possible sort, for the first time I felt quite frankly sick with despair for the Soviet people. That such a potentially super-rich country as ours has been brought to a state of such poverty! It is terrible to think of it.[62]

It is also terrible to think of an America following the same socialist path to ruin.

To damn capitalism is to damn prosperity, abundance, and, ultimately, life itself. If you want to know what capitalism has done for you lately, take a walk to the nearest grocery store and *open your eyes.*

---

62   Chris Anderson, *The Long Tail: Why the Future of Business is Selling Less of More* (New York: Hyperion, 2008), p. 45.

# A Lesson on Censorship

A 2014–15 CONFLICT OVER EDUCATION in a Colorado county offers an opportunity to discuss the meaning and significance of censorship.

Political wrangling between the Jefferson County (Jeffco) teachers' union and the conservative-majority school board set off conflicts in the district, ultimately resulting in the recall of those board members. The focus of student walkouts in numerous Jeffco schools—walkouts that drew national publicity—was a board proposal to appoint a committee to review (among other things) the Advanced Placement U.S. History (APUSH) course.

As the Independence Institute's Ross Izard notes, the original proposal, by board member Julie Williams, was not adopted, and John Newkirk, another of the conservative board members, proposed to strike Williams's "politically inflammatory language" (Izard's words) regarding such things as "respect for authority" and "civil disorder."[63] Nevertheless, the mere fact that Williams proposed a committee to review curricula sparked outrage and the resulting protests.

---

63  Ross Izard, "Jeffco Union Rewrites History, Fuels Protests," *Complete Colorado*, September 29, 2014, http://completecolorado.com/pagetwo/2014/09/29/jeffco -union-rewrites-history-fuels-protests/.

The student walkouts were described, not only by the students themselves but by numerous media outlets and other observers, as "civil disobedience" in response to the board's attempts to "censor" history. But, whatever the problems of Williams's proposal, it certainly was not an effort to "censor" history—and describing it as such obfuscates the meaning of the term and distracts from the very real dangers of censorship.

Given that Jeffco students were mainly protesting a proposed review of a history course, it seems appropriate that they learn the meaning of censorship. Obviously, some of their teachers, as well as various activists and journalists, could use a refresher course as well.

Media reports about the walkouts are filled with accusations that Williams's proposal calls for or amounts to the "censorship" of history. The College Board itself, the private, nonprofit corporation that created APUSH, declares, "The College Board's Advanced Placement Program supports the actions taken by students in Jefferson County, Colorado to protest a school board member's request to censor aspects of the AP U.S. History course."[64] And a media release by the American Civil Liberties Union of Colorado also explicitly refers to Williams's proposal as an attempt at "censorship."[65]

But, regardless of the problems with Williams's proposal, it does not constitute or call for censorship. It arguably calls for or likely would lead to inappropriate board meddling in the teaching of history, but that is not the same thing as censorship—and anyone who claims it is simply does not know (or is intentionally distorting) what censorship means. Both the College Board and

---

64  Nelson Garcia, "The College Board Supports Jeffco Protests," 9News KUSA, September 26, 2014, http://www.9news.com/news/education/the-college-board -supports-jeffco-protests/249879461.

65  "Academic Freedom Groups Oppose 'Deeply Problematic' Jefferson County Curriculum Review Proposal," American Civil Liberties Union of Colorado, October 1, 2014, http://aclu-co.org/academic-freedom-groups-oppose-deeply -problematic-jefferson-county-curriculum-review-proposal/.

the American Civil Liberties Union of Colorado—among many others—are misusing the term censorship, implying that it means something that it does not mean.

Censorship is any government restriction on private speech (broadly understood to encompass all forms of communication), including, within certain limits, private speech on or using government property. So, for example, if government forbids you to say or write something, or to publish a book, that is censorship. If government forbids you to raise funds to produce a political documentary—as the McCain-Feingold censorship law did in some contexts before the Supreme Court substantially overturned it—that is censorship. If government limits the political signs you may place in your yard—as the city of Pueblo did—that is censorship.[66] If government imprisons or executes you for blasphemy, as Middle Eastern Islamic regimes regularly do, that is censorship. If government unreasonably stops you from protesting on "public" (i.e., government-owned) property, that is censorship (although the term "unreasonably" becomes a tricky one to define in that context).

Censorship does not pertain to terms of employment, whether offered by a private company or a government entity.

For example, government school teachers may not deliver racist rants to their classrooms without facing the possibility (and hopefully the reality) of termination of their employment. If a Jeffco teacher attempted to get his students to join a new local chapter of the Ku Klux Klan by passionately advocating the group in class, and the school where he worked fired him on the grounds that his classroom speech was intolerable, neither the College Board, nor the American Civil Liberties Union of Colorado, nor anyone else, would accuse the school of censoring the teacher.

---

66   "Pueblo Ordinance Limits Number of Political Signs on Property," KRDO. com, September 30, 2014, http://www.krdo.com/news/pueblo-ordinance-limits -number-of-political-signs-on-property/28347072.

Nor does censorship refer to the selectivity of course materials in a classroom, whether private or government.

With respect to curricula in the classroom, those are necessarily selective. If a teacher spends a class period covering certain materials, ideas, and sources, the teacher necessarily cannot spend that same period covering other materials, ideas, and sources. For example, I believe Jeffco history teachers would do well to discuss in the classroom the works of Amity Shlaes on the Great Depression. If a history teacher does not use that source, is the teacher thereby "censoring" history? Obviously not. The teacher is simply selecting other sources.

Likewise, the fact that the College Board's "AP Development Committees define the scope and expectations of the [history] course"[67]—which necessarily means that those committees narrow the scope of the course—does not mean that the College Board is "censoring" history by excluding whatever falls outside of the "defined scope" of its course.

So why is it not "censorship" when the College Board decides the "scope" of a history course, but it is "censorship" when the school board seeks to do so? The answer is that it's not censorship in either case. (Ironically, the College Board later altered its APUSH history course in ways that addressed some of Williams's concerns.)[68]

When a school board helps select educational materials for the government schools it supervises, that is by its nature not "censorship." Someone at some level has got to decide which materials are used in a class—and, by implication, which materials are not used. If "censorship" meant any omission of any material,

67 "Course and Exam Description: AP United States History Including the Curriculum Framework," College Board, Fall 2015, http://media.collegeboard.com/digitalServices/pdf/ap/ap-us-history-course-and-exam-description.pdf.

68 Sherrie Peif, "Jeffco Board Vindicated by College Board's Changes to U.S. History Framework," *Complete Colorado*, August 3, 2015, http://completecolorado.com/pagetwo/2015/08/03/jeffco-board-vindicated-by-college-boards-changes-to-u-s-history-framework/.

idea, or source in a government classroom, then every single such classroom would be practicing "censorship" every single day with respect to nearly every material or source ever published.

That said, one may reasonably criticize how government schools select their materials without calling the process censorship. Julie Williams's original proposal, with its vague language about "objectionable materials," about the promotion of "citizenship" and "respect for authority," and about the discouragement of "civil disorder" (among other things), was badly conceived and horribly drafted.[69] For details, see my own critique of Williams's proposal or the letter from the National Coalition Against Censorship to the school board.[70] (Although the issue at hand is not censorship, the letter makes some valid points.)

On the other hand, Williams was seeking to make the teaching of history more inclusive, not less inclusive, at least in some respects. She proposed, "Instructional materials should present positive aspects of the United States and its heritage." Notably, she did not say that instructional materials should not present the negative aspects of history—despite the smears of some of her critics.

Although the exclusion of certain materials in a government classroom does not constitute censorship, inclusion of other materials does constitute a violation of people's rights to speak freely. How so?

As the ACLU recognizes in other contexts, "The Supreme Court has ruled that just as the First Amendment protects an

---

69   See http://www.boarddocs.com/co/jeffco/Board.nsf/files/9NYRPF6DED70/$file/JW%20PROPOSAL%20Board%20Committee%20for%20Curriculum%20Review.pdf (accessed September 12, 2016).

70   Ari Armstrong, "Jeffco's Julie Williams Seeks to Replace One Brand of Activist Teaching with Another," AriArmstrong.com, September 27, 2014, http://ariarmstrong.com/2014/09/jeffcos-julie-williams-seeks-to-replace-one-brand-of-activist-teaching-with-another/; Letter to Ken Witt and the Members of the Board of Education of Jefferson County Public Schools, National Coalition Against Censorship, October 1, 2014, https://www.scribd.com/fullscreen/241615021.

individual's right to say what he or she wants, it also protects his or her right not to say something."[71]

A person has just as much moral right not to speak, and not to support speech of which he disapproves, as he does to speak, and to support speech of which he approves. For example, I have the right to publicly advocate atheism and to help finance a book advocating atheism, and I also have the right not to do those things. If government forced me to promote atheism, that would be a violation of my right to freedom of speech, just as surely as if government forced me not to promote atheism.

What does that imply with respect to the curricula of government schools? When government forcibly takes someone's money—as it does with school taxes—to finance the propagation of ideas or materials of which the taxpayer disapproves, that is a violation of the taxpayer's freedom of speech. Of course, to my knowledge, neither the College Board, nor the American Civil Liberties Union of Colorado, nor the National Coalition Against Censorship, nor any of the teachers or students in Jefferson County's "public" schools, nor any of their cheerleaders in the media, have done anything whatsoever to protest such violations of the freedom of speech.

If nothing else, Jeffco students should learn what censorship is and what it is not. Unless Americans fully and accurately understand the meaning of censorship, they cannot expect to fight it.

---

71 "Students Rights—Pledge Of Allegiance," American Civil Liberties Union of Vermont, https://acluvt.org/pubs/students_rights/pledge.php (accessed August 22, 2016).

# When Politics Corrupts Money

SHOULD POLITICIANS BE PERMITTED TO RESTRICT campaign speech? That is a question Colorado voters faced regarding Amendment 65, a 2012 ballot measure asking politicians to support an amendment to the U.S. Constitution "that allows Congress and the states to limit campaign contributions and spending." (The measure passed, but as of late 2016 a federal amendment remains only talk.)

I presented my case against the measure in a debate with Ken Gordon, a former state senator and director of a group called Clean Slate Now. I argued essentially that it aims to violate people's right to freedom of speech.

In hindsight, I should not have conceded, as I did, that "money corrupts politics" in some cases. True, some interest groups spend money on campaigns in the hope of receiving special government privileges, such as corporate welfare subsidies or coercive "protections" against their competitors. However, to concede that "money corrupts politics" wrongly implies that the modern political system is pure and noble until it is corrupted by money.

The proper way to describe the problem is that, within modern government, politics corrupts money.

Francisco d'Anconia, one of the heroes of Ayn Rand's novel *Atlas Shrugged*, describes the nature of money in his famous speech on the matter:

Money is a tool of exchange, which can't exist unless there are goods produced and men able to produce them. Money is the material shape of the principle that men who wish to deal with one another must deal by trade and give value for value. Money is not the tool of the moochers, who claim your product by tears, or of the looters, who take it from you by force. Money is made possible only by the men who produce.[72]

D'Anconia describes precisely the problem of influence-peddling in government:

Money is the barometer of a society's virtue. When you see that trading is done, not by consent, but by compulsion—when you see that in order to produce, you need to obtain permission from men who produce nothing—when you see that money is flowing to those who deal, not in goods, but in favors—when you see that men get richer by graft and by pull than by work, and your laws don't protect you against them, but protect them against you—when you see corruption being rewarded and honesty becoming a self-sacrifice— you may know that your society is doomed.[73]

Although the source of money is virtuous because it is production, money is corrupted when it is used to buy political favors. When the government is charged, not with protecting the rights of individuals to produce peacefully and trade consensually, but with attempting to control economic activity, the inevitable result is influence-peddling by interest groups.

Gordon inadvertently offered evidence for this when, in the debate with me, he described the lobbying of the insurance

---

72  Ayn Rand, *Atlas Shrugged*, 35th Anniversary Edition (New York: Dutton, 1992), p. 410.
73  Ayn Rand, *Atlas Shrugged*, p. 413.

companies prior to the passage of ObamaCare. The entire framework for such influence-peddling is the leftist vision—which Gordon shares—of a government-controlled health industry. When the government controls health care, lobbying by interest groups regarding health policy inevitably follows.

Amendment 65 was a futile attempt by the statist left to solve the problems created by statist policies. As I argued in my debate with Gordon, the censorship of political speech that Amendment 65 advocates will not solve the problem of influence peddling; it will only make that problem worse. As I pointed out, under Amendment 65, the proposed censorship laws would themselves be crafted by the influence peddlers.

In order to solve the problem of interest groups seeking political favors, we must understand that politics corrupts money, not the other way around, and that the solution is to establish a government that protects individual rights rather than controls economic activity and forcibly transfers wealth.

# Why Forcibly Limiting Campaign Spending is Censorship

OUR RIGHT OF FREE SPEECH AS RECOGNIZED and protected by the First Amendment is a cornerstone of liberty and of America's republican form of government.

That right is under assault, and our freedom of speech is at risk of serious erosion.

In the wake of the *Citizens United* Supreme Court case, which upheld the right of a group of citizens to distribute a documentary criticizing Hillary Clinton while she was a candidate for president in 2008, the "progressive" left has launched a campaign to overturn the First Amendment with a new amendment restricting freedom of political speech.

In 2012, citizens in two states, Montana and Colorado, supported ballot measures requesting the passage of such a constitutional amendment.

The Montana measure, Initiative 166, explicitly seeks to overturn *Citizens United*; asserts that "corporations are not human beings with constitutional rights"; and calls for "limits on overall campaign expenditures and limits on large contributions to or expenditures for the benefit of any campaign by any source, including corporations, individuals, or political committees."[74]

In Colorado (as also discussed in the previous essay), Amendment 65 (originally Initiative 82) calls for "an amendment to the United States Constitution that allows Congress and the states to limit campaign contributions and spending."[75]

Both measures are part of a long-term, nationwide campaign to promote a new amendment limiting the First Amendment. If such an amendment were passed, it would be the first time a portion of the Bill of Rights was intentionally repealed.

Nor is this movement limited merely to the petulant whining of the business-loathing "progressive" left, which detests the *Citizens United* decision upholding free speech. A poll conducted by the Associated Press and the National Constitution Center asked the following question: "Do you think there should or should not be limits on the amount of money corporations, unions and other organizations can contribute to outside organizations trying to influence campaigns for president, Senate and U.S. House?"[76]

Eighty-three percent of respondents said there "should be limits." That such a huge proportion of the American population would overtly call for censorship of political speech is both astonishing and frightening. Unless more Americans can be persuaded to support the right of free speech, censorship is inevitable, putting at risk the American system of constitutionally guaranteed liberty.

---

74  "Ballot Language for Initiative No. 166 (I-166)," Montana Secretary of State, http://sos.mt.gov/Elections/2012/BallotIssues/I-166.pdf (accessed September 12, 2016).

75  Language of Ballot Language for Initiative 82, Colorado Secretary of State, http://www.sos.state.co.us/pubs/elections/Initiatives/titleBoard/filings/2011-2012/82Final.pdf (accessed September 12, 2016).

76  "The AP-National Constitution Center Poll August, 2012," Associated Press and GfK Roper, August 2012, http://ap-gfkpoll.com/main/wp-content/uploads/2012/09/AP-NCC-Poll-August-GfK-2012-Topline-FINAL_1st-release.pdf.

And censorship is precisely what this movement demands. Censorship means that the government may forcibly restrict who may speak, how they may speak, or what they may say.

Consider some of the key implications. The new constitutional amendment as envisioned by both the Montana and Colorado ballot measures would explicitly authorize federal and state politicians to pass legislation limiting campaign spending. In other words, politicians would be charged with silencing their own critics. Prohibiting such tyranny was a major reason the founders drafted and ratified the First Amendment.

Despite the fact that today's left manifestly detests productive, for-profit corporations, corporations and all groups have a moral and constitutional right to express their views and to spend their own resources doing so. The left's endless chant that "corporations aren't people" is true but irrelevant. Like all groups, corporations are groups of individuals, each of whom has rights. As a group of individuals, a for-profit corporation has a right to spend its resources advocating its political or philosophical views. The government's only proper role in this sphere is to recognize and protect that right. The only alternative is for the government to censor corporate speech in violation of the rights of the individuals who compose the corporation.

Consider that many for-profit corporations exist with the explicit aim to publish commentary. For example, the *Objective Standard*, where this article originally appeared, is a for-profit corporation. Not only did this article oppose the ballot measures in Montana and Colorado, but Craig Biddle, the journal's editor, endorsed Mitt Romney for president.[77] The Montana measure explicitly states that Biddle and I have no right to free speech insofar as we write for a corporate-owned publication, whether we write about campaigns or anything else. Indeed, the Montana

---

77  Craig Biddle, "Romney-Ryan 2012—Ayn Rand Forever," *Objective Standard*, August 14, 2012, https://www.theobjectivestandard.com/2012/08/romney-ryan -2012ayn-rand-forever/.

measure asserts that we have no constitutional rights whatsoever insofar as we write for a corporation.

Likewise, many media outlets, ranging from the *Denver Post* to Fox News to MSNBC, are for-profit corporations. Under the proposed laws, all such outlets would potentially be subject to censorship.

Many media outlets are also not-for-profit corporations, including the left-leaning PBS and the right-leaning Watchdog. org (a project of the Franklin Center for Government and Public Integrity). The Montana measure makes no distinction between for-profit and non-profit corporations—all are to be denied their right of free speech.

Of course, under the laws envisioned, Congress and state legislatures could exempt politically-favored groups from government censorship. They could also revoke such exemptions at will. Thus, even if certain media outlets were somehow exempted, the lingering threat of censorship would cause them to second-guess their endorsements and to seek a censor-approved "balance" of coverage.

Even if the government exempted "news" corporations from censorship, the censors would still get to decide what constitutes a "news" corporation. Would the *Objective Standard* qualify? The non-profit corporation Citizens United produced the documentary critical of Hillary Clinton at issue in the legal case. The corporation Obama's America Foundation produced the film *2016: Obama's America*, highly critical of the president and in theaters running up to the 2012 elections. Would these corporations be censored? If not, why not?

If the censorship laws exempted "news" corporations broadly defined, groups not exempted could simply spin off "news" divisions and produce books, films, and "news" papers promoting their political views. Who would be in charge of deciding which community newspaper is a "legitimate" news organization and which was founded to promote particular candidates and political causes?

The *Citizens United* decision illustrates the sweeping scope of censorship laws then under review:

> [T]he following acts would all be felonies. . . . The Sierra Club runs an ad, within the crucial phase of 60 days before the general election, that exhorts the public to disapprove of a Congressman who favors logging in national forests; the National Rifle Association publishes a book urging the public to vote for the challenger because the incumbent U. S. Senator supports a handgun ban; and the American Civil Liberties Union creates a Web site telling the public to vote for a Presidential candidate in light of that candidate's defense of free speech. These prohibitions are classic examples of censorship.[78]

Perhaps under the newly proposed censorship laws the government censors would round up the prohibited books and celebrate with a bonfire.

The censorship laws as proposed by the Montana and Colorado ballot measures would not be restricted to corporations, whether for-profit or non-profit. The Montana measure explicitly says the campaign speech of individuals should be censored; the Colorado measure does not specify the nature, scope, or intended victims of the censorship laws. Thus, all individuals and all groups, including unions and ad-hoc community groups, could fall under the censor's boot as well.

What about the "progressive" claim, as the Montana measure puts it, that "money [is] property, not speech?" The First Amendment is not about the "right" to talk to yourself in your living room. Even those Soviets who survived Stalin's murder machine retained that "right." Rather, the First Amendment protects each individual's right to advocate his beliefs to others, so long as he does not violate rights, including property rights,

---

78 *Citizens United v. Federal Elections Commission*, Supreme Court, January 21, 2010, no. 08–205, https://www.supremecourt.gov/opinions/09pdf/08-205.pdf.

in the process. (For example, I have no "right" to barge into your living room in the middle of the night to make a speech, nor to yell "fire" in a theater when there is no fire.)

One cannot advocate one's beliefs except by expending resources, as by printing pamphlets or books, dialing one's phone, placing a sign in one's yard, purchasing computer equipment, driving to a radio station for an interview, or the like. Censorship by restricting an individual's or a group's expenditure of resources on speech is still censorship.

The First Amendment properly recognizes and protects each individual's right to advocate his beliefs, whether alone or as part of a group. In *Citizens United*, the Supreme Court properly upheld the right of free speech. To preserve the Bill of Rights and America's republican form of government—which critically depends on the liberty to criticize government—Americans must oppose efforts to institute censorship, and they must proudly and loudly champion the right of free speech.

# The Egalitarian Assault on Free Speech

WHY DO SO MANY ON TODAY'S LEFT so forcefully advocate censorship when it comes to campaign spending? Hasn't the left traditionally stood up for free speech, at least in the political realm?

The "progressive" left has always suffered from a basic contradiction: It seeks to protect "civil liberties"—traditionally including the right of free speech—yet it does not recognize property rights, which are essential to all our rights. For example, one has no freedom of speech without the freedom to produce or purchase and then use print copies, internet connections, microphones, broadcast time, and the like.

Indeed, the left enthusiastically embraces the widespread violation of property rights, including the confiscation of wealth to finance the welfare state, in order to promote egalitarianism—that is, government-enforced equality of outcome. Egalitarianism, for example, is at the root of Barack Obama's desire to "spread the wealth around." Even though the left cannot achieve the impossible ideal of perfect equality of outcome, egalitarianism remains its driving motivation.

In recent years, the left's commitment to egalitarianism in the sphere of economics has led it to support censorship in the sphere of political speech. For clear evidence of this, consider the two 2012 state ballot measures asking voters to restrict campaign spending (also considered in the previous essay).

In Montana, Initiative 166 states, "[T]he people of Montana establish that there should be a level playing field in campaign spending, in part by prohibiting corporate campaign contributions and expenditures and by limiting political spending in elections."[79]

In Colorado, Amendment 65 asserts that the government should restrict campaign spending "to ensure that all citizens, regardless of wealth, can express their views to one another and their government on a level playing field."[80] Elena Nunez of Colorado Common Cause, a cosponsor of the measure, said, "Amendment 65 is about leveling the playing field so everyone can be heard regardless of their ability to write huge campaign checks."[81]

The drafters of these censorship measures thus openly state their egalitarian motivation: They wish to forcibly limit the speech of those who have greater resources to make them "level" with those who have fewer resources.

Notice that these measures do nothing whatsoever to improve the ability of the non-wealthy (however defined) to advocate their beliefs. It's not as though these measures seek to impose a special tax on the speech of "the wealthy" in order to subsidize the speech of "the poor." Rather, these proposed censorship laws are purely about forcibly restricting the speech of those with greater resources. The measures thus provide an excellent illustration of the fundamental nature of egalitarianism: It is not essentially

---

79  "Ballot Language for Initiative No. 166 (I-166)," Montana Secretary of State, http://sos.mt.gov/Elections/2012/BallotIssues/I-166.pdf (accessed September 12, 2016).

80  Language of Ballot Language for Initiative 82, Colorado Secretary of State, http://www.sos.state.co.us/pubs/elections/Initiatives/titleBoard/filings/2011-2012/82Final.pdf (accessed September 12, 2016).

81  "Colorado Constitutional Amendment 65: Vote Yes," *Boulder Weekly*, October 4, 2012, http://www.boulderweekly.com/content-archives/voters-guide/vote-2012/colorado-constitutional-amendment-65-vote-yes/.

about helping the less-well-off, but rather about harming the better-off in order to achieve "equality" through destruction.

Contrast the egalitarian vision of equality of speech with the sort of equality envisioned by the Declaration of Independence and the First Amendment: equality before the law. The First Amendment does not guarantee that each speaker will be equally persuasive, or that each speaker will be able to spend the same amount of resources advocating his beliefs. Rather, the First Amendment guarantees the equal right of each individual to speak, as much and as effectively as his abilities and resources allow. The First Amendment does not guarantee, for instance, that an illiterate street bum will be as effective a speaker as a well-educated and wealthy radio personality. The First Amendment is not about "leveling the playing field" in the sense of making all speakers equally effective; it is about establishing equal treatment under the law and prohibiting the government from restricting anyone's (rights-respecting) speech in any way and to any extent.

The proposals to forcibly restrict campaign spending—which means, to impose censorship on political speech—flagrantly violate the principle of equality before the law. They also directly contradict the First Amendment—which is why both the proposals and their advocates seek a new constitutional amendment to overturn the First.

One pretext of the left's egalitarian assault on free speech is the myth that the speech of the wealthy somehow infringes on the speech of the less-wealthy. For example, Elena Nunez and Danny Katz, the cosponsors of the Colorado ballot measure, write, "Amendment 65 tells lawmakers to level the playing field so that everyone has a chance to be heard, not just those with the ability to write $10 million checks."[82]

---

82  Elena Nunez and Danny Katz, "Amendment 65: Voters, Not Money, Should Drive Elections," *Denver Post*, September 27, 2012, http://www.denverpost.com/2012/09/27/amendment-65-voters-not-money-should-drive-elections/.

But the speech of the wealthy in no way restricts the speech of the less-wealthy. To take an example from Colorado, heiress Pat Stryker is worth billions, and she has spent millions in Colorado politics promoting leftist causes and candidates.[83] I have spent a miniscule fraction of that amount advocating my political beliefs in Colorado. Yet nothing Stryker has said, nor all the money she has spent advocating her views, has in any way restricted my ability to speak. Indeed, the only barriers to my speech are the existing campaign censorship laws currently enforced in Colorado. It is the nature of individual rights that they do not conflict when they are recognized and protected. Stryker can exercise her right of free speech fully, and so can I. By contrast, censorship laws necessarily restrict the speech of some for the alleged benefit of others.

Of course, leftists typically pretend that their censorship laws are not actually censorship. For example, Nunez and Katz claim that, under the proposed laws, "The content of speech would remain protected—absolutely—by the First Amendment so that every American could speak his or her mind without fear of government censorship." However, this artificial division between the "content of speech" and the form of speech—in this case, the spending of one's money to promote one's ideas—is absurd. If the government said, "Anyone may say whatever he wishes—the content of speech shall not be restricted—within the privacy of his own home," that would hardly recognize the right to free speech. Obviously restricting people's ability to advocate their beliefs by means of restricting their ability to spend their resources doing so is censorship.

Observe the parallels between egalitarian wealth transfers and egalitarian censorship. Just as egalitarians believe it is inherently unjust for some to earn more than others, so they believe it is

---

83  *Forbes* listed the net worth of Pat Stryker as $1.4 billion in 2012 and $2.6 billion as of August 23, 2016; see http://www.forbes.com/profile/pat-stryker/. *Colorado Peak Politics* has reported on Pat Stryker's political contributions over the years; see http://coloradopeakpolitics.com/tag/pat-stryker/.

inherently unjust for some to spend more promoting their ideas than do others. Just as egalitarians pretend that "the rich get richer while the poor get poorer"—as though in a free market the success of one person necessarily comes at the expense of another—so they pretend that the speech of those with more resources somehow restricts the speech of those with fewer resources. In both cases, egalitarians see the world as a "fixed pie," so the gains of some must impose a loss on others. In reality, when people respect each other's rights, they either leave others alone or benefit from others by consensual exchange.

(A complication in the current debate is that some interest groups spend their resources to seek subsidies and unjust legislation, but in such cases the problem is not with the right of free speech, but rather with the power of government to impose rights-violating laws.)

While today's egalitarian advocates of censorship target campaign spending, by logical implication they should also advocate broader forms of censorship. Various wealthy donors (e.g., Charles Koch) finance not only the campaigns of particular candidates and the promotion of particular measures; they also finance educational programs with the ultimate aim of affecting political change. According to egalitarian premises, there is no reason why the government should not also "level the playing field" by censoring speech when it comes to such educational efforts—which could include speech about philosophy, literature, economics, and so on.

Moreover, on the egalitarian premise that government should assure equal outcomes of speech, there is no reason why government should restrict its censorship to the expenditure of resources. No doubt some speakers are more thoughtful and more eloquent than others. More powerful than a million-dollar check is a rich, captivating voice or an eloquence that resonates with and appeals to listeners. On the egalitarian vision of equality, should not speakers with such voices or abilities somehow be forced not to sound so good or be so articulate? Should not the most persuasive writers be forced to garble their words so as to become "equal" to the less persuasive writers? These are the only ways to genuinely "level the playing field" in the realm of speech, so far as outcomes are concerned.

Those who wish to protect the right of free speech, to save the First Amendment, and to achieve equal treatment before the law must reject egalitarianism in its every form and manifestation. The proper aim of government is not to "level the playing field" by confiscating the wealth of the more productive or restricting the speech of the more persuasive or anything of the sort; rather, it is to protect the equal rights of everyone to live his own life, to control his own property, and to say whatever he wants (consistent with the rights of others) without fear of government interference. The animating principle of justice as recognized by America's founding documents is not equality of outcome, but equality before the law.

# Campaign Laws Throw Common Sense Out the Window

IT IS DECEMBER OF 1787. You hold an intense interest in a revolutionary document, the proposed Constitution for the United States. Will you speak out, or will you remain silent?

Maybe you could write out your thoughts and print them in a pamphlet to distribute in your town. Pamphlets, signed and unsigned, for decades played a crucial role in American political discourse; eventually they would fill such books as *Pamphlets of the American Revolution*. Or you could rent out a room to hold a meeting. You contemplate the opportunities.

Your friend just returned from Pennsylvania, where he witnessed an attack on James Wilson, a key drafter of the Constitution. Eventually this story would become part of the tapestry of Catherine Drinker Bowen's book *Miracle at Philadelphia*. These are tense times. Should you speak out anonymously?

You have heard the debate over the missing Bill of Rights. Would the new federal government protect such cherished liberties as freedom of speech? In just a few years such concerns would give rise to the First Amendment, guaranteeing that "Congress shall make no law . . . abridging the freedom of speech, or of the press; or the right of the people peaceably to assemble."

Now imagine, if you can, the impossible absurdity of some bureaucrat standing up to proclaim, "Anyone wishing to speak out on the proposed Constitution must first register with the proper authorities, then report to those authorities the names and addresses of every significant donor to your cause, as well as all of your significant expenses, as defined by said authorities, on penalty of daily fines, and in accordance with a hundred pages of dense legalese. To assist you with this process, the government will run classes instructing you on the proper way to speak your minds."

Can you imagine how Sam Adams, or John Hancock, or the then-anonymous writers of the Federalist essays, or any of the founders would react to such a demand? The Federalists and Anti-Federalists would momentarily forget their dispute in joint outrage. If he were exceptionally lucky, all that would happen to such a bureaucrat is that he would be tarred and feathered and then run out of town on a rail.

And yet those controls on speech describe the burdens Coloradans now face if they wish to speak out on any ballot measure. And we did this to ourselves. Or, rather, a tyrannical majority, stirred to passion by anti-liberty activists, did it to the minority. In 2002 voters approved Amendment 27, now Article XXVIII of the state constitution, to impose campaign censorship.

For censorship is precisely what the campaign laws accomplish. As several activists told the Secretary of State in 2011 in written and oral comments, the laws in fact prevent some people from speaking out, or speaking out as much, because of the onerous requirements.

At least the Tenth Circuit Court of Appeals ruled in favor of a small activist group that got sued under the campaign laws. Because of this ruling, then-Secretary of State Scott Gessler, who expressed grave concerns about the chilling effect of the campaign laws on free speech, proposed a rule raising the "trigger" spending level for filing as an issue group from $200 to $5,000. (This rule eventually was thrown out by the courts.)

Consider a few of the campaign laws' legion absurdities. If you run a newspaper, you are not subject to the rules. If you print up pamphlets, you are. What if you start up something which to you seems like a newspaper, but which to your political opponents seems like political campaigning? Then you get sued.

If you speak out directly on a ballot measure, you are subject to the rules. If you "educate" the public only about the underlying issues, you are not. At the Secretary of State's meeting, Matt Arnold of Clear the Bench testified to the absurdity of an issue group getting sued by an attack group not subject to the same requirements. Arnold should know: He himself was sued by the laughably named "Colorado Ethics Watch."[84]

On February 14, 1776, an anonymous author put the lie to the left's paranoia about financial influence. He wrote, "Who the author of this production is, is wholly unnecessary to the Public, as the object for attention is the doctrine itself, not the man. Yet it may not be unnecessary to say, that he is unconnected with any party, and under no sort of influence public or private, but the influence of reason and principle."

Today we know the author to be Thomas Paine. The work is *Common Sense*. He merely stated his authenticity, and proved it only through the cogency of his arguments, which he presumed individuals intelligent enough to grasp and independently evaluate.

Yet Colorado's campaign laws throw Common Sense out the window.

---

84  More recently, Arnold has himself been criticized for suing under the campaign laws; see Paul Sherman, "Colorado's Campaign-Finance Bullies Threaten Free Speech," *Denver Post*, August 23, 2016, http://www.denverpost.com/2016/08/23/colorados-campaign-finance-bullies-threaten-free-speech/.

# Ruling Furthers Free Speech

MARKING A SIGNIFICANT VICTORY FOR FREE SPEECH, U.S. district court judge John Kane ruled in 2014 that the Coalition for Secular Government (CSG) need not comply with Colorado's byzantine registration and reporting requirements in order to finance and distribute an issue paper that argues against a statewide ballot measure.

Around that time, CSG released the paper, "The 'Personhood' Movement Versus Individual Rights," which Diana (Brickell) Hsieh and I coauthored.[85] The paper argues (among other things) that the so-called "personhood" measure on Colorado's ballot, Amendment 67, would violate women's rights to seek an abortion, to use the birth control of their choice, and to seek common in vitro fertility treatments. The paper also makes the philosophic case for a woman's right to seek an abortion.

In 2008 and 2010, Hsieh registered CSG with the government and filed reports, as required by Colorado law, in order to finance and distribute previous versions of the paper that opposed "personhood" measures on the ballot in each of those years. Kane's ruling meant that Hsieh did not need to comply with the

---

85 "New Paper: The 'Personhood' Movement Versus Individual Rights," Coalition for Secular Government, October 8, 2014, http://www.seculargovernment.us/a67.shtml.

campaign reporting requirements in 2014. ("Personhood" failed to make the ballot in 2012.)

During the October 3 trial for the case, the government's lawyers defending the campaign finance laws argued (among many other things) that, because Hsieh was effective in speaking out to a broad audience, the government had an interest in forcing her to register and report. Kane brilliantly replied in his October 10 ruling:

> [Is it the case] that the effectiveness of political speech—the fact it resonates, generates interest, and is downloaded from the internet by individuals wanting to read it—somehow elevates or enervates the public's informational interest in its disclosure? The more vibrant the public discourse the more justified the burdening of the speech is? Surely not. It must be remembered by those older than Ms. Hsieh that the internet is the new soapbox; it is the new town square. CSG's "personhood" paper is Tom Paine's pamphlet. It is the quintessence of political speech.[86]

Why is Kane's ruling a victory for free speech? Consider the laws and rules on the books in Colorado dictating what you must do if you wish to speak out for or against any candidate or ballot measure.

If your group consists of two or more people and you spend more than $200, you must understand and comply with a 152-page document and related materials describing the state's campaign finance laws;[87] register with the government; regularly

86  *Coalition for Secular Government v. Scott Gessler,* United States District Court for Colorado, October 10, 2014, https://docs.google.com/file/d/0B6BBPNUKUv KSNDFMc0pacUNDZXdPenMwLUxPaTFvMXlNaUhV/preview?pli=1.

87  As revised in 2015, the document is 140 pages in length; see "Colorado Campaign and Political Finance Manual," Colorado Secretary of State, July 2015, http://www.sos.state.co.us/pubs/elections/CampaignFinance/files/CPFManual.pdf.

report contributions and expenditures to the government; report the names and addresses of contributors who donate $20 or more, and the employers of contributors who donate $100 or more; face the threat of $50 per day in fines for late reports; face the threat of your political opponents dragging you into court for alleged violations of the campaign laws; face the threat of courts imposing substantial civil penalties for technical violations of those laws; and proceed knowing that whatever advice the secretary of state's office offers may well be rejected by courts if you are sued (as happened to an acquaintance of mine).

It's no wonder that a Colorado legislator who supports the campaign finance laws admitted, "Complying with all this is complicated, and really does take a lawyer."[88]

A consequence of the laws is that many people who might otherwise speak out about political matters choose not to do so. I have declined to pursue ideas for producing and distributing political flyers because of the onerous burdens of the campaign laws. And those who do choose to proceed with their political speech face the burdens listed above and are legally forbidden to speak anonymously.

Kane ruled "CSG falls outside the scope of ballot issue-committees to which Colorado's campaign finance disclosure laws may constitutionally apply." Further, Kane awarded attorney fees to CSG, warning "state lawmakers that the Secretary will be on the hook for fees every time a group, like CSG, . . . has to sue to vindicate its First Amendment rights."

Although Kane's ruling is a great victory for CSG and for free-speech rights in Colorado, it is unfortunately very limited in its scope. Consistent with previous court rulings, Kane allows that the government's "informational interest" in requiring campaign reports permits government to restrict freedom of speech in other

---

88  Ari Armstrong, "Morse: Complying with Campaign Laws 'Really Does Take a Lawyer,'" AriArmstrong.com, December 17, 2011, http://ariarmstrong .com/2011/12/morse-complying-with-campaign-laws-really-does-take-a-lawyer/.

cases, particularly when groups speak out about a candidate rather than a ballot measure.

Further, Kane ruled that throwing out the $200 reporting threshold in favor of a higher one was beyond the scope of his authority. (He didn't even consider eliminating the requirements.) By way of background, the Tenth Circuit Court previously ruled that there is no "bright line below which a ballot issue committee cannot be required to report contributions and expenditures," and the secretary of state's recommendation to raise the reporting threshold to $5,000 was thrown out by the courts. Further, the Colorado Supreme Court declined to clarify the scope of Colorado's campaign finance laws when Kane asked it to do so.[89] In response to the legal uncertainty caused by this series of court decisions, Kane wrote:

> The nature of CSG and its advocacy render any "informational interest" the government has in mandating contribution and expenditure disclosures so minimal as to be nonexistent, and certainly insufficient to justify the burdens compliance imposes on members' constitutional free speech and association rights.
>
> This conclusion is so obvious, moreover, that having to adjudicate it in every instance as the Colorado Supreme Court implies is necessary itself offends the First Amendment. By setting in stone the uncertainty that precipitated this litigation in the first place, the Court's interpretation chills robust discussion at the very core of our electoral process. I am without authority, however, to undo the damage done. . . . The wholesale invalidation of Colorado's $200 contribution threshold for ballot issue

---

89  Sarah Lee, "Federal Judge Asks for Clarification of Colorado Campaign Finance Laws," Center for Competitive Politics, October 2, 2012, http://www .campaignfreedom.org/2012/10/02/federal-judge-asks-for-clarification-of -colorado-campaign-finance-laws/.

committees, though warranted, would go beyond my charge and be improvident.

Kane continued in a passage and an endnote:

> [T]his state of affairs means that no precedent has been established and the stability this matter of considerable public importance so needfully requires will have to await another day or days and even more lawsuits. . . . I suggest the "post hoc, case-by-case review" mandated by the Colorado Supreme Court majority is itself unconstitutional. . . . The sheer expense and delay of unnecessary litigation chills, if not freezes entirely, prospective speakers' resolve to exercise their First Amendment rights and should be mitigated with due haste.

The result is that other groups can only guess whether courts will require them to comply with the campaign finance laws.

Nevertheless, Kane's decision offers relief to CSG and likely to similar groups, and Kane's pointed language brings much-needed attention to important aspects of the continuing injustices of Colorado's campaign finance laws.

Congratulations to Hsieh and to her attorneys, Allen Dickerson and Tyler Martinez of the Center for Competitive Politics, for winning this important victory. And kudos to Judge Kane for ruling in favor of free speech in this case and for eloquently speaking out against continuing infringements of free speech.

# Questioning the Welfare State

THE WELFARE STATE IS IN CRISIS. The promises made in its name are a mixture of wishful thinking and outright lies. It emerged as a mechanism of power; it displaced, crowded out, and crushed voluntary and participatory institutions; it enervated and atomized societies and undercut personal responsibility; it substituted dependency and patronage for independence and rights. In usurping from citizens responsibility for their own welfare, it has turned them into clients, vassals, subjects, supplicants. —Tom G. Palmer (*After the Welfare State* [p. 52])[90]

The modern welfare state began to take shape in the 1880s in Otto von Bismarck's Germany, and it took off in the United States in the 1930s under Franklin Delano Roosevelt's "New Deal." Now that the welfare state is thoroughly entrenched throughout most of the world, is there any reason to question its existence or any way to eliminate it? There is a reason and a way, and these are the subjects of the essays in *After the Welfare State*.

---

90   Tom G. Palmer, ed., *After the Welfare State* (Ottawa, IL: Jameson Books, 2012). Parenthetical notations in this essay refer to that book.

The book, published by Jameson Books in conjunction with Students for Liberty and the Atlas Network,[91] features nine essays covering the history of the welfare state and some of the common criticisms of it. The publishers of the book intended it to be short (with only 136 pages for the essays), inexpensive (easily downloaded or shipped in bulk paperbacks), and readily available and accessible to college students. These qualities make the book a fine introduction to the history and problems of the welfare state.

In "Bismarck's Legacy" (the fourth essay in the book), Tom G. Palmer (who also edited the book) recounts the Prussian roots of the welfare state. Dependency, writes Palmer, is not an "unintended consequence" of the welfare state; it is its primary objective: "All welfare states begin by rejecting the classical liberal principles of limited government and individual freedom. They create systems of political control over the behavior of constituencies through deliberately induced dependence, typically justified through one doctrine or another of collective identity and collective purpose" (p. 37). Or, in the words of Bismarck himself, the father of the modern welfare state: "Whoever has a pension for his old age is far more content and far easier to handle than one who has no such prospect" (p. 35).

After reviewing the Prussian origins of the welfare state, Palmer shifts to U.S. history and to FDR, who also wanted to make people easier to handle. The welfare state, writes Palmer, took an especially tragic turn in the 1960s under the so-called "Great Society."

> The result was not quite what was promised, as the proliferation and expansion of programs targeted to the poor, and most significantly, to black Americans, resulted in social meltdown, the hollowing out of American cities, the withering of the voluntary organizations of

---

91  Students for Liberty offers a free download of the book at http://studentsforliberty.org/after-the-welfare-state/.

civil society, the evisceration of the two-parent family, rising crime rates, and unprecedented levels of youth unemployment. (pp. 42–43)

Today, writes Palmer, given the huge budget deficits faced by governments throughout Europe and the Americas, "It's the end of the road for the welfare state" (p. 52). That is the theme of several other essays in the book as well. Piercamillo Falasca offers a depressing account of the damage wrought by the Italian welfare state; Aristides Hatzis does the same for Greece. Michael Tanner (of the Cato Institute) adds a brief review of the status of welfare statism in Europe and the United States, invoking frightening statistics concerning government spending, deficits, and unfunded liabilities.

To me, the most fascinating part of the book is a pair of essays on the history of mutual aid societies, written by two leading scholars in the field. David Green discusses the history and importance of such societies in Britain; David Beito reviews the comparable history within the United States.

Green describes the basic purpose of the societies:

In Britain the friendly societies were the most important providers of social welfare during the nineteenth and early twentieth centuries.

The friendly societies were self-governing mutual-benefit associations founded by manual workers to provide against hard times. They strongly distinguished their guiding philosophy from the philanthropy which lay at the heart of charitable work. The mutual benefit association was not run by one set of people with the intention of helping another separate group; it was an association of individuals pledged to help each other when the occasion arose. (pp. 55–56)

Green and Beito explain the value of these societies, which individuals voluntarily joined and maintained, and which provided services such as life and health insurance. The authors also show that government regulations of the societies' activities, along with competition from coercively funded government welfare programs, helped drive most mutual aid societies out of existence.

On the whole, *After the Welfare State* is an excellent primer on the history and problems of the modern welfare state. Unfortunately, the book does not deliver on its implied promise to describe how to end the welfare state and institute voluntary institutions in its place.

And, unfortunately, the book is ambivalent about whether it even advocates the abolition of the welfare state. Palmer concludes his first essay confidently: "We need to end the welfare state" (p. 14). Not all of the contributors to the book agree. For example, Hatzis writes that "perhaps" the government ought to intervene "carefully when there is a market failure" (p. 23), and later he explicitly advocates a welfare state, albeit a reformed one: "a safety net [only] for the misfortunate poor" rather than one that provides "lavish benefits for the [politically] powerful and the wealthy" (p. 30).

In his final essay, Palmer backs off from his confident call for the abolition of the welfare state, arguing instead that classical liberals (a group of which he considers himself a member) reasonably disagree about the role of government-issued welfare. Palmer writes in his concluding lines:

> Classical liberal thinkers, despite often robust disagreement among themselves, have agreed that the creation of more wealth is the solution to the alleviation of poverty and that, because outcomes are not themselves generally subject to choice, just and efficient institutions are the key to increasing wealth and diminishing poverty. Moreover, although many make room for state provision of assistance to the poor and indigent, all agree that there is a hierarchy of means for the alleviation of poverty, cascading from personal responsibility and self-help, to

mutual aid, to charity, to the least preferred option, state compulsion. (p. 136)

Thus, Palmer suggests, even though he personally wants to "end the welfare state," his is merely one opinion among many, and he is not prepared to definitively rule out a welfare state.

Those looking for a consistent defense of individual rights will not find it in *After the Welfare State*. But those seeking to learn the basic history of the welfare state and some of the major problems with it will find the book a worthy resource.

# The Integrity of Condemning
# Social Security While Collecting It

IN AN ABSURD ACT OF INJUSTICE, the left routinely castigates those who criticize government redistribution programs while accepting some benefits of those programs.

For instance, writing for the *Huffington Post*, Michael Ford blasts those on the right who allegedly hold the attitude, "venerated in public, disdained in private"; he describes such people as "VIP-DIPers."[92] Ford proceeds to smear Ayn Rand with the term because she accepted Social Security and Medicare payments—after being forced for most of her working life to pay into those rights-violating programs. According to Ford, Rand accepted those "benefits" even as she "said it was wrong for everyone else to do so" (a flagrant misrepresentation of Rand's position). Ford concludes, "In the end, Miss Rand was a hypocrite. . . ."

Similarly, commenting prior to the Republican convention in 2012, David Sirota wrote for *Salon*:

---

92  Michael Ford, "Ayn Rand and the VIP-DIPers," *Huffington Post*, December 5, 2010, http://www.huffingtonpost.com/michael-ford/ayn-rand-and-the-vip -dipe_b_792184.html.

Hysterical jeremiads against "socialism" and for the "free market" are sure to pepper the Republican convention, if not from the dais then from the assembled rabble. . . . [Y]ou can expect the assembled media to loyally echo the themes—and barely notice that the paroxysm of anti-government hysteria is taking place inside a socialist enterprise.

That's right, as the Daily Dolt first noted, "The stadium where the GOP will be announcing 'We Built This!' was financed primarily by the government." Specifically, according to Marquette University's National Sports Law Institute, "The total budget for the project was $139 million, of which public money accounted for $86 million and team money accounted for $53 million."[93]

Sirota thus implies that, if one uses a tax-financed stadium, not only can one not properly oppose the tax financing of the stadium, one cannot justifiably condemn socialism or promote free markets.

One more example: In 2012 Eli Stokols reported for Denver's Fox31:

Mitt Romney's Colorado campaign held an event involving local business owners expressing their outrage over President Barack Obama's statement that businesses "didn't build" their companies themselves.

"It pissed me off," said Jack Davis, who hosted the press conference . . . at Advance Surface Technologies, which he bought 15 years ago. "To me, that statement really demonstrates to me that the president doesn't have an appreciation for what it takes to start and run a business."

93  David Sirota, "The Four Biggest Convention Stories You Won't Hear About," *Salon*, August 29, 2012, http://www.salon.com/2012/08/29/the_four_biggest _convention_stories_you_wont_hear_about/.

Like the business owner who hosted the Romney campaign's "We Did Build That" event Monday in Colorado Springs, Davis acknowledged that he did receive a government-backed SBA loan.[94]

This story led to predictable smears. Lynn Bartels, then a reporter for the *Denver Post*, Tweeted, "Great reporting by @EliStokols on the 'You didn't build that' double standard."[95] The leftist publication *Colorado Pols* asked, "[A]t what point will people stop the fake rage against the evil 'government' when *they knowingly take advantage of government programs?*"[96]

In short, these leftists shrilly mock, "You hypocrite! You accept money the government is handing out, yet you dare criticize the government for handing out money!"

Never mind the fact that the government looted Rand's paycheck for most of her life to finance rights-violating "entitlement" schemes. Never mind the fact that the government forcibly took people's wealth to build the stadium in question (thereby driving private investment from the market) and that government continued to seize wealth from anyone doing business near the stadium. Never mind the fact that Davis was forced—by threat of criminal prosecution and imprisonment— to subsidize government loans long before he ever applied for one. To leftists, such facts do not matter. What matters to them is that government be free to hand out wealth without anyone recognizing where the wealth came from or criticizing the government for expropriating that wealth.

---

94  Eli Stokols, "Local Business Owners Spar for Romney, Obama Over 'You Didn't Build That,'" Fox31, July 31, 2012, http://kdvr.com/2012/07/31/using -local-business-owners-romney-obama-campaigns-spar-over-you-didn/.

95  Lynn Bartels, July 31, 2012, https://twitter.com/lynn_bartels/ status/230448144993906689.

96  The article in question, originally published at http://coloradopols.com/ showDiary.do?diaryId=18218, is not available as of August 24, 2016.

A message someone posted to Facebook illustrates the absurdity of smearing critics of government programs for drawing some benefit from those programs: "Saying that Rand was a hypocrite for benefiting from social security . . . is like saying people who opposed communism were hypocrites for benefiting from government issue clothing." Or, as I wrote a couple years ago, "According to the logic of [leftists], somebody standing in a Soviet bread line has no right to criticize Soviet bread lines, because he is after all waiting his turn for the bread."[97]

Consider the implications of the left's smears. According to the left's "logic," the bigger the government program—the more wealth distribution it entails—the less legitimate is any criticism of the program. Today, we are forced to finance government roads, government schools, and myriad government "entitlement" and handout schemes. By the left's "reasoning," if a person drives on government roads (that he is forced to fund), sends his children to government schools (that he is forced to fund), or "benefits" from any government assistance program (that he is forced to fund), then he is a hypocrite for criticizing those programs.

The implication is that, if the government forcibly confiscated every last cent of your income, making you dependent on the government for your every scrap of food and rag of clothing, you would have no moral right to criticize the government whatsoever.

Such is the utter inanity of today's left, which claims that the victims of government rights violations cannot complain about those violations because and to the extent that the victims are victimized.

Ayn Rand offered a retort to such absurdities in her 1966 essay, "The Question of Scholarships" (in the book *The Voice of Reason*). Although Rand here specifically addresses tax-subsidized

97 Ari Armstrong, "Would Perlmutter Also Lambast Soviet Bread Line Critics?," AriArmstrong.com, October 18, 2010, http://ariarmstrong.com/2010/10/would-perlmutter-also-lambast-soviet-bread-line-critics/.

scholarships, her reasoning applies to all cases of recouping some of one's wealth taken for government programs:

> The recipient of a public scholarship is morally justified *only so long as he regards it as restitution and opposes all forms of welfare statism.* Those who advocate public scholarships, have no right to them; those who oppose them, have. If this sounds like a paradox, the fault lies in the moral contradictions of welfare statism, not in its victims.
>
> Since there is no such thing as the right of some men to vote away the rights of others, and no such thing as the right of the government to seize the property of some men for the unearned benefit of others—the advocates and supporters of the welfare state are morally guilty of robbing their opponents, and the fact that the robbery is legalized makes it morally worse, not better. The victims do not have to add self-inflicted martyrdom to the injury done to them by others; they do not have to let the looters profit doubly, by letting them distribute the money exclusively to the parasites who clamored for it. Whenever the welfare-state laws offer them some small restitution, *the victims should take it.*[98]

Contrary to the smears of the left, there is no contradiction or lack of integrity in condemning a rights-violating government program that one is forced to finance, while simultaneously recouping some benefit from that program. To forego the

---

98  Ayn Rand, "The Question of Scholarships," in *The Voice of Reason* (New York: Signet, 1988), p. 42. Regarding Social Security, critics might argue that one does not recoup one's own money (if retired) but rather collects the money of current contributors. To this I have a two-part response. First, if a person declined Social Security benefits, that would not decrease the payroll taxes for anyone; the funds would be sucked up by government spending in some form. Second, one's children and friends almost certainly would rather their taxes go to people they know and like, so for a person to decline benefits would harm the person's loved ones.

opportunity to recoup some of one's stolen money would be to compound the injustice.

The victims of right-violating government programs should proudly and righteously condemn those programs—and seek to minimize the injustice of the programs by recouping whatever value they can from them. Far from hypocrisy, this is an act of integrity: recognizing the full truth and upholding one's principles accordingly.

# Nation Needs Shared Liberty, Not Sacrifice

BARACK OBAMA HAS CALLED FOR "SHARED SACRIFICE" to address the nation's debt. But forcing individuals to sacrifice their present and future wealth to politicians' whims caused the problem. To restore economic prosperity, we need to stop sharing sacrifices and start sharing a respect for liberty and people's rights.

Obama's appeal depends on a basic confusion about the nature of sacrifice. The term shares the same root as sacred. Historically, a sacrifice involves a religious rite of giving a gift, often a slaughtered animal, to some deity. That's where we get the term sacrificial lamb. When viewed in this light, "shared sacrifice" presents an obvious problem: Somebody plays the role of the lamb.

Over time sacrifice in popular usage came to mean giving up anything. But because so many things can be given up, and for so many different reasons, the term lost any clear meaning. Instead, often it functions to cloud people's thinking.

Some use the term to mean giving up something minor to get something better. Chess players call surrendering a piece to get ahead in the game a sacrifice. In baseball, a player makes a sacrifice bunt to allow a teammate to advance a base, though the hitter returns to the bench. In these cases, making a "sacrifice" is good for you: The narrow or short-term loss increases your odds of winning in the end.

Consider the student who stays home to study, rather than going to the movies or the mall, to earn a good education and career. Or a mother who cuts her own budget to expand the opportunities for the children she dearly loves. Or a soldier who risks his safety to defend his liberty and home. Or a fundraiser who supports medical research in memory of a loved one. Should we call these "sacrifices," even though the person achieves a greater value?

In other cases people use the term sacrifice to mean giving up something important for something trivial or even evil. Someone may sacrifice his career for a drinking binge, his marriage for a meaningless affair, or his savings account for a night of gambling. In extreme cases, various cultures murdered people for human sacrifices to appease some make-believe god, worship a ruler, or try to mystically gain the victim's strength.

When people apply the same term to earning a good job through hard work and slitting somebody's throat, that reveals a fundamental confusion.

So what does Obama mean by a "shared sacrifice?" He wants us to imagine that each of us needs to hit a sacrifice bunt so Team America can win the economic game. What he really means is that he wants to sacrifice the time, labor, and earnings of some people for the benefit or pleasure of his political supporters.

Obama clearly favors tax hikes. From the left we hear envious snarls to further loot "the rich." Proposals on the table include raising tax rates for some and eliminating tax breaks for things like mortgages and health insurance, for the purpose of raising net taxes. (It's fine to dump tax deductions for special groups, but only to lower rates generally.)

A tax involves forcibly seizing people's wealth, usually for the benefit of some special interest. Ultimately, Obama threatens to send armed federal agents to your house to drag you off to prison to make you share in this sacrifice.

Other aspects of Obama's "shared sacrifice" involve reducing sacrifice, not increasing it. CNN writes of a farmer "sympathetic to the president's calls for shared sacrifice, even if that means cuts to ethanol subsidies."[99] But a subsidy entails forcibly looting other taxpayers. Eliminating the subsidy means halting the sacrifice of some Americans to others. We're all for that!

If sacrifice means forcing some individuals to surrender their hard-earned wealth to others, then our goal should be to eliminate sacrifice entirely. A society that sacrifices some people to others relies on brute force and rampant injustice.

A civilized society does not demand sacrifices. Instead it protects people's rights, including their right to control their own wealth and property as they see fit. In a civilized society, people interact by voluntary consent, not coercion.

"Shared sacrifice"—forcibly looting some for the benefit of others—caused the debt crisis. The solution is to phase out shared sacrifice, not expand it. We should dramatically cut federal spending to balance the budget and then start paying off the debt.

If we care about solving the debt crisis and restoring America's economic strength, if we care about protecting the rights of each individual, then we must reject shared sacrifice and instead demand shared liberty.

---

99  Adam Aigner-Treworgy, "President Obama Listens to Farmers in Rural Illinois," CNN, August 17, 2011, http://whitehouse.blogs.cnn.com/2011/08/17/president -obama-listens-to-famers-in-rural-illinois/.

# The Crucial Distinction Between Subsidies and Tax Cuts

How many times have you heard a tax cut described as a "subsidy?"

It's bad enough that government forcibly confiscates our wealth for the purpose of transferring our money to others in the form of welfare (whether regular or corporate). Adding insult to injury, pundits and politicians often speak as though letting a person keep his own money is the equivalent of handing him someone else's money. They use the terms "tax cut" and "subsidy" interchangeably.

For example, the *New York Times* ran an editorial under the headline, "Subsidize Students, Not Tax Cuts," as though handing students other people's money is no different than letting producers keep their own money.[100]

Unfortunately, even some advocates of free markets use the terms interchangeably. For example, economist David Friedman argues that a subsidy and a tax credit for a given activity "differ only in labeling." Friedman continues, "They have the same

---

100   "Subsidize Students, Not Tax Cuts," *New York Times*, April 24, 2012, http://www.nytimes.com/2012/04/25/opinion/subsidize-students-not-tax-cuts.html.

effect on the federal budget. They provide the same amount of subsidy."[101] James Wilson of Downsize DC agrees.[102]

In a variant of this linguistic contortion, some claim that paying for some government project or welfare program is the equivalent of "paying for" a tax cut. For example, in an article for CNN, Jeanne Sahadi writes that Mitt Romney "has failed to specify which tax breaks he'd eliminate or reduce to help pay for his proposed tax cuts."[103] Greg Sargent makes the same claim for the *Washington Post*.[104]

In a 2012 speech, Barack Obama mocked his congressional opponents, describing their proposals as follows: "Their basic idea is that if we spend trillions of dollars more on tax cuts . . . the benefits then will spread to everybody else."[105] Thus he equates government spending with tax cuts, as though there were no difference between the government handing taxpayers' money to automakers or food stamp recipients and the government reducing the amount of money it forcibly seizes from producers.

David Harsanyi sensibly replied to such nonsense, "We don't 'pay' for tax cuts, Mr. President, we pay for spending."[106]

---

101  David Friedman, "What the Tea Party Gets Wrong," August 10, 2011, http://daviddfriedman.blogspot.com/2011/08/what-tea-party-gets-wrong.html.

102  James Wilson, "Are Tax Breaks Really Subsidies?," Downsize DC, August 12, 2011, https://www.downsizedcfoundation.org/blog/are-tax-breaks-really-subsidies.

103  Jeanne Sahadi, "Obama vs. Romney on Taxes," CNN Money, July 5, 2012, http://money.cnn.com/2012/07/05/news/economy/obama-romney-taxes/.

104  Greg Sargent, "Romney: No Need to Detail How I'll Pay for Massive Tax Cuts; Just Trust Me," *Washington Post*, June 17, 2012, https://www.washingtonpost.com/blogs/plum-line/post/romney-no-need-to-detail-how-ill-pay-for-massive-tax-cuts-just-trust-me/2012/06/17/gJQAJi4IjV_blog.html.

105  "Remarks by President Obama at Poland, OH, Campaign Event," *Daily Kos*, July 6, 2012, http://www.dailykos.com/story/2012/07/06/1106869/-Remarks-by-President-Obama-at-Poland-OH-campaign-event-July-6-2012.

106  David Harsanyi, "We Don't 'Pay' for Tax Cuts, Mr. President, We Pay for Spending," *Human Events*, July 10, 2012, http://humanevents.com/2012/07/10/we-dont-pay-for-tax-cuts-we-pay-for-spending/.

The effect of this abuse of concepts is to obfuscate the difference between the wealth that an individual produces and owns and the wealth that the government forcibly seizes and redistributes. If the term "subsidy" refers to government distribution of wealth forcibly seized from producers, then it logically cannot refer to a reduction in what the government forcibly seizes from producers.

The cognitive effect of using the same concept to refer to both things is to obliterate the difference between the two in people's minds. The political effect is that when the government allows us to keep even a single dollar of our own money, this is regarded as a "subsidy."

So let us clear the conceptual field. Properly speaking, a "subsidy" means the government giving wealth that it forcibly seized from individuals or businesses to other individuals or businesses. Examples include corporate bailouts, tax-supported loans, and Social Security payments. A "tax cut" means reducing the amount of wealth the government forcibly seizes from individuals or businesses.

Clarifying the distinction between subsidies and tax cuts is an act not only of conceptual integrity but of justice toward the producers of wealth.

# The Moral Case Against
# Minimum Wage Laws

THE LEGALLY MANDATED MINIMUM WAGE is an economic issue, of course; but it is more fundamentally a moral issue. Unfortunately, usually only the statist left, with its claims about the alleged fairness of higher minimum wages, talks about the moral dimensions of the policy. That needs to change.

Obviously, as of late 2016, minimum wage laws are a big deal politically. Various states and localities have higher minimum wages than the national level.[107] In Colorado, we're looking at a ballot measure to raise the hourly minimum wage to $12 by 2020.[108] We already have a higher minimum wage than federal law mandates, and it's indexed to inflation. One of the big fights between Bernie Sanders and Hillary Clinton was whether to raise the federal minimum wage to $15 or "only" $12. Donald Trump,

---

107   "Minimum Wage Tracker," Economic Policy Institute, August 24, 2016, http://www.epi.org/minimum-wage-tracker/.

108   Aldo Svaldi, "$12 Minimum Wage Measure Makes Colorado Ballot," *Denver Post*, August 15, 2016, http://www.denverpost.com/2016/08/11/minimum-wage-colorado-ballot-initiative-101/.

as we might expect, has flip-flopped over whether he wants to increase the federal minimum wage or leave it the same.[109]

I can think of no politician today who vocally advocates the repeal of minimum wage laws, even though that is still a fairly common position among free-market economists. The reason for this, I think, is that advocates of economic liberty have largely ceded the moral high ground on the issue. Today the usual view is to see anyone who calls for the repeal of minimum wage laws as a cold-hearted bastard who wants to see children starve in the streets. But that's all wrong.

What are the moral issues at stake? I see three main ones.

## 1. It is wrong to forcibly prevent someone from negotiating a salary at which he or she can find a job and is willing to work.

The moral debate is, of course, bounded by economic realities. If we could pass a magic law that would result in everyone getting paid at least $15 per hour (or $100 per hour) without making anyone worse off, no one would oppose it. For people who live in reality, the debate is a little more complicated.

No sane economist would claim that a sufficiently low minimum wage (say, $3 per hour) would increase unemployment. At the same time, no sane economist would deny that a sufficiently high minimum wage (say, $30 per hour) would cause dramatic job loss.

The academic debate largely revolves around the employment effects of relatively modest changes in minimum wage laws. Minimum wage-change deniers aside, this much is clear: Any increase large enough to substantially boost many people's wages

---

109  Michelle Ye Hee Lee, "A Guide to All of Donald Trump's Flip-Flops on the Minimum Wage," *Washington Post*, August 3, 2016, https://www.washingtonpost .com/news/fact-checker/wp/2016/08/03/a-guide-to-all-of-donald-trumps-flip -flops-on-the-minimum-wage/.

is also large enough to throw some people out of work and to chill future creation of certain jobs.

Ultimately, almost no employer is going to keep an employee around who loses money for the business. If Alison, a business owner, can make more money by laying off Benjamin than by paying him $12 per hour (or whatever the law says), then Benjamin goes to the unemployment lines. For each employee and each job, there is an upper pay boundary beyond which an employer will not go. (I'm assuming here that no one is crazy enough to suggest that government force employers to hire people at a loss.)

If the minimum wage is set at $12 per hour, then a person who can contribute only $11 per hour to a business will not find work. The real minimum wage is zero,[110] and minimum wage laws force people to accept zero rather than even a penny below the legal minimum.

Nor is such legally mandated unemployment justified by utilitarian concerns. One could argue, for example, that if total wage gains surpass total wage losses due to cut jobs, then that would be a net benefit. Or one could argue that total wage increases would have to outweigh losses by some multiple. But such calculations do not justify forcibly harming some people by outlawing their employment.

People are individuals, not averages, and individuals have rights— including the right to engage with others by mutual consent.

## 2. Minimum wage laws treat entry-level, unskilled, and other low-paid workers as incompetent to manage their

---

110   Many people have used the line "the real minimum wage is zero." Various people attribute the line to Thomas Sowell; whether or not he was the first to use it, it appears in Thomas Sowell, "Minimum Journalism," *Jewish World Review*, August 1, 2001, http://www.jewishworldreview.com/cols/sowell080101.asp.

**own affairs and negotiate their own contracts without the intervention of politicians and bureaucrats.**

For many people, a minimum wage job is an entry-level job, the first step on a long path of career advancement. As the Bureau of Labor Statistics reports for 2015, "Although workers under age 25 represented only about one-fifth of hourly paid workers, they made up about half of those paid the federal minimum wage or less."[111]

A person does not earn only money on the first job; he or she earns invaluable experience. One critical skill that people need to learn is how to negotiate employment contracts with employers. Minimum wage laws essentially communicate, "Don't worry about thinking carefully about what you can contribute to a business and what your time is worth to employers, and don't worry about standing up for yourself at work; we the elites will take care of your pay negotiations for you."

In some cases, especially for young professionals, the compensation *is* the work experience, which is why many people sign up to work for free as interns when they are legally allowed to do so.

Some people seek out a side-job, sometimes with low pay, to supplement a family's income. This group can include teens and young adults living at home who want extra pocket money while going to school, spouses who split time between kids and work, and people in semi-retirement. Around two-thirds of all minimum wage workers are part-time (although not always by preference).[112] David Neumark finds that many minimum wage workers contribute to greater household income, one

---

111  "Characteristics of Minimum Wage Workers, 2015," Bureau of Labor Statistics, Report 1061, April 2016, http://www.bls.gov/opub/reports/minimum -wage/2015/home.htm.

112  Drew Desilver, "Who Makes Minimum Wage," Pew Research Center, September 8, 2014, http://www.pewresearch.org/fact-tank/2014/09/08/who-makes -minimum-wage/.

reason why, at a $10.10 minimum wage, around half of the
financial gains would go to families over twice the poverty line,
while around a third of the gains go to families over triple the
poverty line.[113]

In the name of fighting poverty, minimum wage laws can
interfere with the job choices of people who are not poor. Some
employers respond to a higher minimum wage by eliminating or
never offering certain jobs; some demand that employees become
more productive during each paid hour. Minimum wage laws
communicate, "We're from government, and we know best:
You may not negotiate a lower wage based on the expectation
of assuming fewer responsibilities, having more flexibility, or
enjoying less stress while at work."

Then there are some people who really are trying to support
a family on a single minimum wage income. That's a tough
situation, no doubt. The best path out of that situation is not to
work the same entry-level job for a little more pay; it is to build
more-marketable skills and get a better job.

Bear in mind that the main problem is not that some heads of
households make only the minimum wage; it is that, in most poor
families, no one works at all.[114]

Rather than "help" struggling families by violating people's
rights and throwing some people out of work, government should
respect people's rights to cooperate consensually with others and
to decide how to dispose of their own wealth. For example,
government should repeal job-killing licensure laws starting with

113   David Neumark, "Reducing Poverty via Minimum Wages, Alternatives,"
Federal Reserve Bank of San Francisco, December 28, 2015, http://www.frbsf
.org/economic-research/publications/economic-letter/2015/december/reducing
-poverty-via-minimum-wages-tax-credit/.

114   Ibid.

the most obviously irrational ones, such as laws requiring hair braiders to undergo hundreds of hours of pointless instruction.[115]

Forced wealth transfers violate people's rights (a large issue to pursue further elsewhere); however, even momentarily granting the assumptions of welfare statists, minimum wage laws are a bad approach. Targeted welfare addresses the problem it's intended to solve (at least superficially) without directly disrupting the labor market.[116]

It is telling that some people would rather increase the minimum wage than, say, repeal the 15.3 percent federal payroll tax, which is extremely damaging to the poor. For such activists, government taking more control of people's lives seems to be the point.

Of course, private efforts to help the poor can be morally appropriate and economically sensible; for example, people who wish to do so can contribute to charities that help people on low incomes get on their feet and improve their job skills.

So far, we have focused on the employee and job seeker. Next we turn to the other side of the employment relationship and our third reason why minimum wage laws are immoral.

## 3. It's wrong to force employers to pay more than they can negotiate on a free market.

The employer often is the "forgotten man" or woman in policy debates about the minimum wage, but let's not forget who actually creates the jobs in question. It ain't the politicians or the street activists.

---

115   See "Braiding," Institute for Justice, http://ij.org/issues/economic-liberty/braiding/ (accessed September 3, 2016). For a broader look at licensure laws, see Dick M. Carpenter II, Lisa Knepper, Angela C. Erickson, and John K. Ross, *License to Work*, Institute for Justice, May 2012, http://ij.org/wp-content/uploads/2015/04/licensetowork1.pdf.

116   See Matt Zwolinski, "The Minimum Wage is a Bad Tool for Fighting Poverty," *Bleeding Heart Libertarians*, April 4, 2016, http://bleedingheartlibertarians.com/2016/04/the-minimum-wage-is-a-bad-tool-for-fighting-poverty/.

The premise of the "fairness" argument for minimum wage hikes seems to be that employers easily could afford to pay their employees more, but they just refuse. Most people with such presumptions have never actually tried to run a business or make payroll. In the real world, most businesses fail within ten years.[117] In the real world, many business owners run losses some years. Those who think it's easy to run a business and pay low-skilled employees high wages are welcome to try.

Employers are not society's beasts of burden, to create higher-paying jobs out of thin air as demanded by those who create no jobs. (Even politically subsidized projects are funded ultimately by private-sector producers.) Employers, no less than employees, have rights—including the right to engage with others by mutual consent.

Every dollar a business pays in expenses has to come from somewhere. If a business owner pays one employee more, that money has to come out of others' pay, facility expansion, job training, computer upgrades, higher prices paid by customers, or the like. A business owner has a moral right to negotiate freely with the various suppliers, employees, and customers of the business in ways the owner judges best for the business overall.

Employers do not create the problem that some people can demand only a (relatively) low wage. Employers help solve that problem by helping employees develop marketable skills.

When people have more marketable skills, employers have to pay them more, or employees quickly find better terms elsewhere. That's why only a small fraction of people earn the federal

117 "Business Employment Dynamics," Bureau of Labor Statistics, April 28, 2016, http://www.bls.gov/bdm/entrepreneurship/entrepreneurship.htm.

minimum wage and why only about one in five employees would be directly affected by a $12 minimum wage.[118]

In the main, people don't make more money because government says they must; they make more money because they become more productive. People become more productive primarily with better capital—the best-educated person in the world with access only to a shovel will produce very little. Capitalists, not politicians, are why people on average increased their earnings from $4,200 in 1900 to $33,700 in 1999 (both figures using 1999 dollars).[119] At a given time, some people earn relatively more than others because they can persuade employers that they can produce relatively more wealth for the business.

Minimum wage laws scapegoat employers for problems that they did not cause. And those laws forcibly interfere with employers' efforts to address the problems, as an indirect consequence of running their businesses, by offering people the opportunity to gain work experience.

In short, minimum wage laws treat low-wage employees as though they needed a government nanny and employers as though they deserved a government yoke. These laws violate the rights of employers and employees alike. On moral grounds, minimum wage laws should be repealed, not expanded.

118   "Characteristics of Minimum Wage Workers, 2015," Bureau of Labor Statistics, Report 1061, April 2016, http://www.bls.gov/opub/reports/minimum-wage/2015/home.htm; David Cooper, "Raising the Minimum Wage to $12 by 2020 Would Lift Wages for 35 Million American Workers," Economic Policy Institute, July 14, 2015,   http://www.epi.org/publication/raising-the-minimum-wage-to-12-by-2020-would-lift-wages-for-35-million-american-workers/.

119   Donald M. Fisk, "American Labor in the 20th Century," Bureau of Labor Statistics, January 30, 2003, http://www.bls.gov/opub/mlr/cwc/american-labor-in-the-20th-century.pdf.

# The Morality of Unequal
# Pay for Unequal Work

THE GOOD NEWS, AS DAN MITCHELL REPORTED in 2012, is that
a measure to force greater "equality" between the pay of men
and women—the so-called "Paycheck Fairness Act"—"didn't get
enough votes to overcome a procedural objection" in the Senate.[120]
The bad news is that this statist measure made it to the Senate
in the first place—and that it is seriously advocated by various
politicians and activist groups.

Mitchell points to an article by Christina Hoff Sommers that
explains the economic problem with the proposal:

> Groups like the National Organization for Women insist
> that women are being cheated out of 24 percent of their
> salary. The pay equity bill is driven by indignation at this
> supposed injustice. Yet no competent labor economist
> takes the NOW perspective seriously. An analysis of more
> than 50 peer-reviewed papers, commissioned by the

---

120  Dan Mitchell, "So-Called Paycheck Fairness Act Would Allow Government
to Second-Guess Private Markets," June 9, 2012, https://danieljmitchell.wordpress
.com/2012/06/09/so-called-paycheck-fairness-act-would-allow-government-to
-second-guess-private-markets/.

Labor Department, found that the so-called wage gap is mostly, and perhaps entirely, an artifact of the different choices men and women make—different fields of study, different professions, different balances between home and work.[121]

As Sommers further explains, the Act would subject employers to class-action lawsuits of unlimited proportions for ambiguous "harms" such as permitting the "lingering effects of past discrimination." The resulting legal chaos, Sommers predicts, likely would lead to "federally determined occupational wage scales"—that is, federal wage controls across the board.

Unfortunately, neither Sommers nor Mitchell offers a principled defense of individual rights in this context. Sommers suggests that the measure is not a "common-sense equity" bill and therefore should be ruled out. Mitchell argues that the core issue is that "we want resources to be allocated by market forces instead of political edicts."

The fundamental principle properly governing this issue, however, is that individuals have the right to control their property as they see fit and to contract with others on a purely voluntary basis. The government's proper job is to protect such rights—not to violate them by meddling in the agreements of consenting adults.

Even if some portion of the "gender gap" in pay were shown to be due purely to gender (one article suggests that part of the problem is that some women are not as aggressive in asking for

121  Christina Hoff Sommers, "The Case Against the Paycheck Fairness Act," American Enterprise Institute, May 6, 2012, http://www.aei.org/publication/the-case-against-the-paycheck-fairness-act/.

raises),[122] that would not justify federal intervention. It might justify individual women asking for raises if they want more money.

Usually a rational employer will offer "equal pay for equal work." Usually doing so keeps employees happier and enables employers to retain good staff. An employer who underpaid women (or any other group) due to prejudice would suffer economically by losing talent to competitors who compensate on the basis of ability. Of course, employers should also offer unequal pay for unequal work—as judged by the employer. (For obvious reasons "Unequal Pay for Unequal Work!" doesn't strike the left as a worthy chant.)

But employers are not morally bound to pay the same wages to employees doing the same work. If one person is willing to perform a job for less money, an employer sensibly offers him less money—just as a consumer sensibly pays less to have the lawn mowed or to have a pair of shoes repaired, if someone will do the same job for less.

Government is morally sanctioned only to protect rights—in this case, to ensure that contracts are reached consensually, without the use of force or fraud; government has no moral sanction to generate outcomes that some people deem "fair." Whenever government seeks to guarantee "fair" outcomes, rather than the equal protection of individual rights, it necessarily violates rights and inevitably generates unfair outcomes.

The government should protect rights and otherwise leave other matters of fairness to the free choices of individuals who associate on strictly voluntary terms.

---

122  "I Work for a Large Multinational Tech Company; I Regularly Hire Woman for 65% to 75% of what Males Make . . . ," *Reddit*, June 9, 2011, https://www .reddit.com/r/TwoXChromosomes/comments/hvv2m/i_work_for_a_large _multinational_tech_company_i/.

# Hobby Lobby and Equal Rights

ALTHOUGH MANY OF THE CRITICISMS of the Supreme Court's 2014 *Hobby Lobby* ruling stem from indefensible premises—such that some people have a "right" to force others to pay for their birth control—other criticisms point to a real problem with the decision and with the law on which it is based, the Religious Freedom Restoration Act (RFRA). The problem is that, although the decision and the RFRA protect the rights of people with particular religious convictions to act in accordance with their own judgment, the decision and Act do not protect the same rights for everyone else.

The proper solution to this legal contradiction is not, as many critics of the Supreme Court's decision claim, for government to stop protecting the rights of people with particular religious convictions. Rather, the proper solution—the approach consistent with the principle of individual rights—is for government to start protecting the rights of all individuals to act on their judgment, which means (among many other things) the right to operate their businesses as they see fit and to voluntarily contract with others—or not to do so—as they see fit.

Consider the case of ObamaCare's requirement that businesses provide to employees health insurance that covers birth control—the matter at the heart of the *Hobby Lobby* decision. The owners of Hobby Lobby do not wish to provide such insurance because they believe certain types of birth control act as abortifacients, and they believe, on faith-based, religious grounds, that abortion is inherently wrong.

But many other people do not want to provide or to purchase such insurance, not because it violates some religious taboo, but because such insurance makes no rational or economic sense. For example, my wife and I are atheists who think abortion should be legal. But we'd rather pay directly for birth control as needed than pay higher insurance premiums to "cover" it. Many women don't even need birth control. By forcing people to buy health insurance that "covers" birth control, government effectively forces some people to subsidize the birth control of others, through higher insurance premiums.

So the pressing question is: Why does the government protect the right of Hobby Lobby's owners to decide what type of insurance to offer, but government does not protect the rights of my wife and me to decide what type of insurance to seek?

Law professor Sasha Volokh discusses such problems with the RFRA.[123] He argues that the law (at least as interpreted) violates the Establishment Clause of the First Amendment, because it recognizes people's rights to act on deeply held religious beliefs, but not people's rights to act on "deeply held secular convictions."

As Volokh notes, former Supreme Court justice John Paul Stevens saw the same problem with the RFRA. In Justice Stevens's words, it "provided the Church with a legal weapon that no atheist or agnostic can obtain." Unfortunately, Stevens wrongly implied that, because government should treat everyone equally under the law, government should violate the rights of religious people along with the rights of atheists and agnostics.

The case about which Stevens wrote involved a Catholic church that wanted to improve its property while local

---

123  Sasha Volokh, "Is RFRA Unconstitutional?," *Washington Post*, July 1, 2014, https://www.washingtonpost.com/news/volokh-conspiracy/wp/2014/07/01/is-rfra -unconstitutional/.

government, for the sake of preserving "historic landmarks," forbade such improvement.[124] But government has no moral right to violate people's property rights for the sake of preserving "historic landmarks" or for any other reason. Those who own property have a moral right to use it as they see fit (so long as they do not violate anyone else's rights in the process), and they have this right whether they want to use their property for religious or nonreligious purposes.

Similarly, in her dissent to the *Hobby Lobby* decision, Ruth Bader Ginsburg concludes that, because the RFRA protects people motivated by certain religious views but not people motivated by other views, government should not protect the rights of any business owner to decide what type of health insurance to offer.[125] Her argument is essentially this: Because government fails to protect the rights of all, it should protect the rights of none. The obvious alternative—and the morally correct one—is for government to recognize and protect everyone's rights fully and equally.

There is no clash between government protecting people's rights and government treating everyone equally under the law. Indeed, ultimately government can treat everyone equally under the law only by consistently recognizing and protecting everyone's rights.

The problem with the recent Supreme Court ruling is not that it recognized the rights of Hobby Lobby's owners to operate their business as they see fit in the sphere specified. The problem is that it does not recognize the rights of everyone—people of faith and people of reason—to operate their businesses and to run their lives as they see fit in all spheres.

124  *City of Boerne v. Flores*, no. 95-2074, Legal Information Institute, June 25, 1997, https://www.law.cornell.edu/supct/html/95-2074.ZO.html.

125  *Burwell v. Hobby Lobby*, no. 13-354, Supreme Court, June 30, 2014, https://www.supremecourt.gov/opinions/13pdf/13-354_olp1.pdf.

# On the Right Not to Bake a Cake

ALTHOUGH A CAKE BAKER OUGHT NOT DISCRIMINATE against gay couples for being gay, he nevertheless has a moral right to do so. This is an application of the right to property—the right to use the product of one's effort as one sees fit. Correspondingly, government has no moral right to force a cake baker (or anyone else) to do business with a gay couple (or anyone else).

Unfortunately, Colorado government (like various other governments) now violates the rights of business owners to operate their businesses as they see fit in this regard. And the *Denver Post* editorial board is happy about that:

> Sometimes the rights guaranteed to individuals collide in uncomfortable ways. The conflict over whether a Lakewood baker [Jack Phillips of Masterpiece Cakeshop] was justified in refusing to make a wedding cake for a gay couple is one of those conflicts.

> We were glad to see the state's Civil Rights Commission . . . uphold a prior ruling that the baker was wrong in turning away Charlie Craig and David Mullins.[126]

---

126  "Bakers Have to Sell to Everyone," *Denver Post*, May 30, 2014, http://www .denverpost.com/2014/05/30/bakers-have-to-sell-to-everyone/.

In addition to being wrong, the editorial's language is imprecise: The so-called Civil Rights Commission did not rule that "the baker was wrong" (he was in fact wrong); rather, it ruled that government will punish the baker if he does not bake cakes for gay couples. There is a world of difference between a private individual condemning some action as immoral and the government punishing that action. Of all potential immoral acts, government should prohibit only a small subset of them: specifically, those that violate rights—which means those involving the use of initiatory physical force (including fraud and the like).

The *Post*'s claim that a gay couple has a "right" to force a baker to bake them a cake—and that this is a "collision" of rights—indicates that editorial's authors have no idea what rights are.

Rights are moral principles defining a person's proper freedom of action in a social context.[127] Rights derive from man's need to pursue life-promoting values; his basic means of identifying and pursuing such values is his own reasoning mind; and a necessary condition for acting on his judgment is his freedom to use the product of his effort as he sees fit. This latter gives rise to the right to property.

That business owners have property rights means that they have a moral right to operate their business as they see fit (provided they respect others' rights)—and that no one, including government, has a moral right to force them to do otherwise.

The actual collision in this case is between one man's moral right to run his business as he sees fit, and the government's illegitimate use of force to stop him from acting on his judgment. That is not a *collision* of rights, it is a *violation* of rights—a violation perpetrated by the government.

Rights properly understood cannot collide. Either a person has a right to a given action or use of specific property, or he does

---

127  Ayn Rand, "Individual Rights," *Ayn Rand Lexicon*, http://aynrandlexicon .com/lexicon/individual_rights.html (accessed August 25, 2016).

not. If he does, no one else can have a right to violate that right. However we evaluate the baker, the government in this matter is in the wrong.

# Businessmen Should Never "Put Moral Judgments Aside"

After Colorado bureaucrats ruled that government may punish a professional cake baker for refusing to bake wedding cakes for gay couples, the *Denver Post* editorialized, "If you invite the public to patronize your cake shop, you have to be prepared to put moral judgments aside and serve all those who walk through your doors."[128]

The *Post* is wrong. To rationally operate their businesses in the pursuit of profit, producers must exercise moral judgment in every aspect of their operations, including the crucial matter of deciding whom to work for and whom to serve. To the degree that producers "have to" act against their moral judgments in some way, that is only because government forces them to do so, thereby violating their rights to operate their businesses according to their own judgment.

It is absurd to suggest, as the *Post* does, that opening one's business to the general public somehow obligates one to serve

---

128  "Bakers Have to Sell to Everyone," *Denver Post*, May 30, 2014, http://www .denverpost.com/2014/05/30/bakers-have-to-sell-to-everyone/.

every individual who walks through the doors, regardless of context. Must a cake baker bake a "God Hates Fags" cake for the bigoted Westboro Baptist Church, or a swastika cake for a neo-Nazi group? Must a restaurant manager ignore his moral judgments and serve every drunken, unruly lout who walks through the doors? Must the *Denver Post* publish "all those" op-ed submissions that come through its doors, regardless of how poorly written, absurd, or ideologically corrupt they are? Obviously not.

Of course there is a big difference between immorally discriminating against a gay couple (as the baker in question did) and morally discriminating against the Westboro Baptist Church. The fact that individuals have a moral right to act according to their own judgment (so long as they do not violate the rights of others by initiating physical force or by committing fraud) does not mean that their moral judgments will always be correct.

At issue is not the fact that the Colorado baker was wrong to discriminate against a gay couple, but the fact that the baker has a moral right to operate his business as he sees fit, and the government has no moral right to punish him for doing so. It is worth pointing out here that when government can forcibly stop producers from acting on their objectively wrong moral judgments, it can—and inevitably will—forcibly stop them from acting on their objectively correct moral judgments.

Contrary to the *Denver Post's* absurd remarks, every aspect of a rational producer's efforts is governed by his moral judgments. When a rational business owner starts a business and decides to enter a particular field, he does so based on his moral judgment that the pursuit is the best way for him to foster his life and happiness. When a rational business owner hires an employee, he does so based on his moral judgment that the employee is a good person suited to the job. When a rational business owner decides to do business with someone, he does so based on his moral judgment that the exchange will prove to be mutually beneficial, and based on his assumption that he is not aiding an immoral cause.

As for producers who act on irrational rather than rational judgments, so long as they do not thereby initiate force, they are no threat to anyone, and they will suffer in a free market to the degree of their irrationality. Just as a business owner has a moral right to decline to do business with someone, so a customer has a moral right to decline to seek out a business's goods or services (for example, people have a moral right to boycott bigoted businesses). And rational producers, seeing an opportunity to make a profit, will rush to earn the business that might otherwise go to irrational competitors.

Neither producers nor consumers should ever "put moral judgments aside," as the *Denver Post* urges; rather, they should seek to act always by their rational, moral judgments. As for government, it has no legitimate business punishing a producer, whether rational or irrational, unless he has somehow violated rights.

# Religious Freedom Laws vs. Equal Protection of Rights

THE PROBLEM WITH RELIGIOUS FREEDOM laws (such as Indiana passed in 2015) is not that they may allow private parties to discriminate against homosexuals; it is that they legally discriminate against nonreligious people. They carve out special legal status for religious people and thus violate the basic principle that government morally must treat all individuals equally under the law.

That said, the proper solution is not to repeal protections of the rights of religious people; it is to extend the same protections to all individuals via generalized law. Consider an analogy. If a government taxed atheists at a higher rate than it taxed religious believers, that would be horribly unjust, but it would also be unjust to tax all believers at the higher rate. The proper solution would be for government to treat all people equally by lightening the tax burden of atheists, thereby moving in the direction of fully respecting people's rights to their wealth. Likewise, regarding religious freedom laws, the proper solution is not for government to violate the rights of religious people as severely as it violates the rights of everyone else; it is for government to stop violating the rights of everyone else, too.

With religious freedom laws, does government protect the rights of religious people to a greater extent than it protects the rights of nonreligious people? Consider two major aspects of religious freedom laws, starting with potential discrimination by private parties against gays.

Critics of Indiana's law as originally passed "feared [it] would have allowed discrimination [by private parties] against the lesbian, gay, bisexual and transgender community," as *USA Today* reports.[129] (Cato's Roger Pilon agrees that's what the law would do, although apparently the measure merely explicitly stated what broader law already implicitly allowed.)[130] In response to widespread criticism, Indiana lawmakers agreed to "fix" the law by nullifying this aspect of it; "Indiana Republicans . . . announced sexual orientation and gender identity will be explicitly protected in the new law" as amended, *USA Today* reports. Governor Mike Pence signed this "fix" on April 2.

The leftist website *Media Matters* argues that the original Indiana law was unique among religious freedom laws in America in that it was the only one that allowed private parties to discriminate against gays.[131] If that's right, now that Indiana's law has been revised, no religious freedom law in the country allows private parties to discriminate against gays.

However, as German Lopez reports for *Vox*, private discrimination against homosexuals is de facto legal in twenty-eight other states that "don't have civil rights laws that would prohibit discrimination against LGBT people in the workplace,

129  Tony Cook, Tom LoBianco, and Doug Stanglin, "Indiana Governor Signs Amended 'Religious Freedom' Law," *USA Today*, April 2, 2015, http://www .usatoday.com/story/news/nation/2015/04/02/indiana-religious-freedom-law-deal -gay-discrimination/70819106/.

130  Roger Pilon, "Indiana's 'Defense' of Religious Liberty," Cato Institute, March 29, 2015, http://www.cato.org/blog/indianas-defense-religious-liberty.

131  Carlos Maza, "Megyn Kelly's Misinformed Defense Of Indiana's Anti-Gay 'Religious Freedom' Law," Media Matters, March 30, 2015, http://mediamatters .org/blog/2015/03/30/megyn-kellys-misinformed-defense-of-indianas-an/203095.

housing, and public accommodations (hotels, restaurants, and other places that serve the general public). It's not the religious freedom laws that allow discrimination; it's the lack of civil rights laws [sic]."[132] Ironically, then, with the latest legal change, Indiana has now outlawed private discrimination against homosexuals whereas before such discrimination was legal.

The main question in this regard, then, is do private parties have a (moral) right to discriminate against homosexuals by denying them service? Or, conversely, do homosexuals have a (moral) right to have government force private businesses to serve them?

Note that the basic legal question is not whether it is immoral to discriminate against homosexuals because of one's religious beliefs. The proper purpose of government is not to outlaw everything some citizens deem immoral; if government attempted to do so, it would achieve a fascist police state on the order of *1984*. Rather, the proper purpose of government is to outlaw violations of individual rights (a narrow range of immoral acts, specifically, those involving the initiation of physical force) and to act only to protect rights.

Although it is immoral for private parties to discriminate against homosexuals by refusing them service or the like, such denial of service violates no one's rights. Rights are not merely what some group or government says they are; rights are objective principles recognizing people's proper freedom of action in a social context.[133]

Each individual has a right—whether or not government recognizes it—to the product of his effort and to freedom of association. A "right" to the product of someone else's effort—

---

132   German Lopez, "Think Indiana is bad? It's Legal to Deny Service to Gay and Lesbian People in 29 States," *Vox*, April 1, 2015, http://www.vox .com/2015/4/1/8325585/lgbt-nondiscrimination-laws.

133   Ayn Rand, "Individual Rights," *Ayn Rand Lexicon*, http://aynrandlexicon .com/lexicon/individual_rights.html (accessed August 25, 2016).

whether a wedding cake, a pizza, an automobile, or an Internet cable—would inherently violate the producing party's rights of property. It would also violate a business owner's freedom of association by forcing him to associate with (i.e., serve) those whom he does not want to associate with. Government's proper role here is to protect individuals' rights to property and association even when they behave immorally, not to force bigoted business owners to serve gays. (Of course, individuals also have a right to denounce and boycott businesses of which they disapprove.)

Regarding religious freedom laws, government ought not give religious people special exemptions to use their property and to associate as they see fit; rather, government should equally recognize the rights of *all* individuals to do so.

The second major aspect of religious freedom laws is that they protect religious people from government abuses. It is well and good to protect religious people from government abuses; however, the law should equally protect all people from such abuses. Ultimately, there should not be religious freedom laws; there should just be laws that protect everyone's freedom.

Mollie Hemingway offers some examples of government abuses in an article for the *Federalist*. Consider her first example:

> Just a few weeks ago, on March 10, the federal government returned the eagle feathers it had seized nine years prior from a Native American religious leader and famed feather dancer Robert Soto. [It is illegal even to possess certain feathers in the United States without special government permission.] He had appealed the seizure of the eagle feathers, for which he faced 15 years in a federal penitentiary and a $250,000 fine, on Religious Freedom Restoration Act grounds.[134]

---

134  Mollie Hemingway, "Meet 10 Americans Helped By Religious Freedom Bills Like Indiana's," *Federalist*, March 30, 2015, http://thefederalist.com/2015/03/30/meet-10-americans-helped-by-religious-freedom-bills-like-indianas/.

It is good that the federal government did not steal Soto's feathers or lock him in a metal cage for fifteen years for possessing feathers; Soto's possession of feathers obviously violates no one's rights. But why should only religious people be protected from such egregious violations of their rights by government? *Every* individual should be so protected. An individual shouldn't have to believe some irrational religious creed in order not to be assaulted by government.

Groups do not have rights, whether a group of homosexuals or a group of religious people. Rights pertain to individuals, and government has a moral responsibility to recognize the equal rights of all individuals. Although it would be wrong for government to violate the rights of religious people more severely than it does already, ultimately religious freedom laws should not exist. They should be replaced with freedom laws—laws that establish freedom for everyone equally.

# Amnesty for Rights-Respecting Illegal Immigrants

IN THE 1850s IN AMERICA, it was illegal to help slaves escape to freedom. In the 1940s in Germany, it was illegal to harbor Jews from the Nazis. In such cases, it can be moral to break the law, and it is immoral to punish people for breaking such laws.

People or governments who violate people's rights under the pretext of law cannot legitimately excuse themselves by saying, "The law's the law." When the law is evil, morally it may be broken, and those who break it deserve amnesty, not punishment.

Yet, when it comes to immigration, many conservatives—even those who call for the protection of rights in other contexts—pretend that illegal immigrants must be punished for the "crime" of seeking to better their lives. Why? Because "the law's the law." Even Thomas Sowell, who usually advocates liberty, advocates such punishment.[135]

Who are these people whom conservatives seek to punish? In many cases, they are people who sought to immigrate to America

---

135 Thomas Sowell, "Amnesty Lite Is Still Amnesty," Creators Syndicate, June 12, 2014, https://www.creators.com/read/thomas-sowell/06/14/amnesty-lite-is-still-amnesty.

so that they could earn better pay for their work or avail themselves of better opportunities for themselves or their families. In some cases, they are people who escaped oppression or tyranny in their homelands. And, in some cases, they are people who, had they not made it into America, would have suffered severe hardship, political or religious persecution, or even death.

On what moral premise should such people be punished? Certainly not on any rational moral premise. Anyone who recognizes and upholds a rational morality—that is, the morality of rational self-interest—must consequently recognize and uphold the propriety of seeking to live where one can live best, or, as the case may be, simply to live.

According to rational morality, rights-respecting foreigners have a moral right to move where they choose and to seek work where they choose, and Americans have a moral right to hire and otherwise associate with such people. These rights are instances of the rights to "life, liberty, and the pursuit of happiness": Each individual has the right to live his life for his own purposes and by his own judgment (so long as he does not violate the rights of others), to live free of the initiatory force of others, and to pursue his happiness as he deems best.

This does not mean that criminals or terrorists have a "right" to immigrate to America; they do not. Nor does it mean that immigrants have a "right" to welfare; they do not. Nor does it mean that immigrants necessarily should be granted citizenship; citizenship is properly a separate matter from immigration. Rather, it means that people who are not known to pose a threat to Americans have a moral right to immigrate to America—and that rights-respecting people who immigrate here illegally deserve amnesty, not punishment.

When conservatives claim that rights-respecting immigrants should be punished for breaking rights-violating immigration laws, they effectively claim that one violation of an immigrant's rights deserves another. Such a position is morally indefensible.

# A Rights-Respecting
# Immigration Policy

ALTHOUGH IN TODAY'S CONTEXT QUESTIONS regarding immigration are complex matters involving the welfare state, laws governing citizenship, threats of cross-border crime and terrorism, and various other issues, the proper principle guiding any thinking about immigration is—as with every political issue—that of individual rights. With that in mind, let's explore some of the various misconceptions about a rights-respecting immigration policy.

**Myth:** "A rights-respecting immigration policy permits criminals and terrorists to enter the country."

**Reality:** Obviously, to protect the rights of its citizens and residents, government must keep out criminals and terrorists— and respond with appropriate defensive force if such are found among immigrants already here. Far from calling for unguarded borders, a rights-respecting immigration policy calls for government to tightly control the borders, with specific legal points of entry and screening processes, allowing in only people whom the government has no reason to believe pose any threat to U.S. citizens.

**Myth:** "A rights-respecting immigration policy entails government provision of welfare to immigrants and permits them to squat on public or private lands."

**Reality:** To protect the rights of citizens and residents, government must not compel them to subsidize immigrants and must not permit immigrants to squat on government or private property. If an immigrant is unable to support himself or unable to find a sponsor willing to support him, government may properly deport him.

**Myth:** "A rights-respecting immigration policy requires government to grant citizenship to immigrants."

**Reality:** Policies pertaining to immigration properly are distinct from those pertaining to citizenship. A rights-respecting government need not ever grant immigrants or their children citizenship; although, in certain cases, granting an immigrant citizenship may be perfectly appropriate. (The proper criteria for citizenship is a complex matter beyond the scope of this post.)

**Myth:** "Support for a rights-respecting immigration policy entails support for any and all proposals claiming to offer immigrants 'amnesty.'"

**Reality:** The principle of individual rights does not tell us whether to support some particular piece of mixed legislation—whether involving amnesty or anything else—which in some ways protects rights and in other ways violates them. Matters regarding mixed proposals for legislation must be assessed with respect to the kinds and degrees of rights violations involved. This is true not only of mixed legislation pertaining to immigration, but of all mixed legislation. To take another example, the fact that the principle of individual rights implies that Social Security must be repealed does not mean that every proposal claiming to move in that direction is necessarily a good proposal.

**Myth:** "A rights-respecting immigration policy requires open immigration during wartime emergencies, regardless of the context."

**Reality:** A wartime emergency may require that government cut off some or all immigration for the duration of the emergency—it depends on the context. For instance, in the context in which Israel exists today, Israelis face a continual barrage of terrorist attacks, rockets, and suicide bombers, and the country morally must take actions with respect to that specific context. In Israel's situation, certain limitations on immigration may be mandatory. However, the fact that Israel is justified in restricting immigration on the grounds that it faces such continual threats does not imply that the United States—which is not in that same situation—should refrain from screening would-be immigrants and permitting entry to rights-respecting individuals.

In summary, regardless of the complexities in establishing a rights-respecting immigration policy, individuals have rights, and government ought not violate the rights of citizens to hire, host, or otherwise associate freely with immigrants; nor should it violate the rights of rights-respecting people seeking entry to the Land of Liberty.

# Government Destroys Buckyballs, Assaults the Mind

IT FELT LIKE CHRISTMAS HAD COME EARLY when I got my package of Buckyballs in the mail. Buckyballs are small, super-strong spherical magnets made of the rare earth metal neodymium. A set of 216 Buckyballs fits comfortably in the palm of your hand.

I stared amazed as I formed the balls into a long string and held one end in the air, the rest of the balls held in place by nothing but their magnetic attraction. The company that makes Buckyballs, Maxfield and Oberton, states, "The arrangement of electrons in rare-earth elements lets them develop strong magnetic fields." No kidding! Then I fashioned the balls into a snowflake pattern. Others have built elaborate structures with multiple sets of the balls.

Buckyballs, I soon discovered, are toys for the mind. They are a thinking person's toy. How can you play with them and not wonder about the chemical nature of rare earth metals (something about which I know hardly anything), and the nature of magnetic forces, and the sheer technological genius that goes into producing these little balls?

Obviously Buckyballs are adult toys, and Maxfield and Oberton emphatically warns users not to give them to children, eat them, inhale them, or place them near objects (such as pacemakers) that are sensitive to magnets. However, for those who use Buckyballs with common sense and due care, they are reasonably safe—just like countless other objects in or around the home from hammers to knives to sugar to prescription drugs to firearms to bicycles to automobiles.

What has been the government's response to Buckyballs? Has it been to recognize the outstanding productive achievements of the company that makes them? To leave the company in peace to conduct its business? Of course not. The government has put Maxfield and Oberton out of business so far as Buckyballs are concerned. The sets I ordered are among the last that will be produced, ever.

Maxfield and Oberton states on its web page, "You've heard about our ongoing battle with the CPSC [Consumer Product Safety Commission]. Due to their baseless and relentless legal badgering, we've sadly decided to stop production of Buckyballs and Buckycubes. We still have a few thousand sets in stock, but once we sell through those, they're gone for good." The company relates the sad story on its web page and in a letter from CEO Craig Zucker.[136] The government declared Buckyballs to be unsafe—which is the same thing as declaring adults to be too stupid and irresponsible to use them safely.

In its complaint, the CPSC reports that some parents have left stray Buckyballs around the house, and toddlers have eaten them. Moreover, some "tweens and teenagers" have attempted to "mimic piercings of the tongue, lip or cheek," and then have

---

136  Some of the relevant material is archived at https://web.archive.org/web/20121227090302/http://www.getbuckyballs.com/save-our-balls and https://web.archive.org/web/20120826104143/http://www.getbuckyballs.com/letter-from-ceo/.

"unintentionally inhaled and swallowed" them. In some cases this has required surgery.[137]

In other words, because a few parents irresponsibly let their toddlers eat Buckyballs, and because a few teenagers stupidly stick them in their mouths or noses despite the warning labels, Maxfield and Oberton is forbidden to sell Buckyballs and we are forbidden to buy them—regardless of whether the company issues clear and explicit warnings with each package, regardless of whether would-be customers are willing to purchase and use the toys in accordance with their own best judgment, and regardless of whether would-be customers have children in their home or office.

"The U.S. Consumer Product Safety Commission . . . is charged with protecting the public from unreasonable risks of injury or death," the government organization states. However, in a rights-respecting country, the government recognizes the right of every adult to decide which risks he deems reasonable. The government's only proper role is to protect rights, such as by overseeing private lawsuits and criminal investigations of rights-violating actions.

The unanswered question is, who will protect Americans from the risks posed to our lives, liberties, and happiness by rights-violating government regulators?

---

137   "CPSC Sues Maxfield & Oberton Over Hazardous Buckyballs® and Buckycube™ Desk Toys," U.S. Consumer Product Safety Commission, July 25, 2012, https://web.archive.org/web/20120805044946/http://www.cpsc.gov/cpscpub/prerel/prhtml12/12234.html?.

# Should Prostitution Be legal?

SOMETIMES GOVERNMENTS BAN ACTIVITIES that are not vices, such as practicing homosexuality, coloring a pooch pink,[138] taking marijuana for medical purposes, or buying alcohol on Sundays.[139] Widespread support exists for ending such uses of political force.

But prostitution normally is a vice. Should government therefore ban it? The proper purpose of government is to protect people's rights, not prevent vice beyond that context. Legal vices include drinking too much alcohol, smoking, overeating, watching too much TV, engaging in indiscriminate sex, and cheating on one's spouse.

Which is worse—that New York Governor Eliot Spitzer hired a prostitute or that he cheated on his wife?[140] I regard Spitzer's

---

138   Mike McPhee, "Boulder Says No to Pink Poodle," *Denver Post*, http://www .denverpost.com/2008/03/10/boulder-says-no-to-pink-poodle/.

139   It was illegal to sell alcohol in stores in Colorado until 2008. See Tim Hoover, "Sunday Alcohol Sales Set," *Denver Post*, April 14, 2008, http://www.denverpost .com/2008/04/14/sunday-alcohol-sales-set/.

140   For some of the details regarding this scandal, see "Spitzer Prostitute Details: $80,000 Spent, Mood Music, Multiple Prostitutes, Up To A Decade Of Use And An Ever-Present Security Detail," *Huffington Post*, August 14, 2008, http://www .huffingtonpost.com/2008/03/12/spitzer-prostitute-detail_n_91116.html.

infidelity as the far worse moral sin, yet that's not what triggered a criminal investigation, wiretaps and possible criminal charges.

You may legally buy an adult a $300 dinner and then take the person home for consensual sex. Or you may legally take the person on a $4,300 weekend getaway for sex. But it's a crime for Spitzer to pay $4,300 directly for sex.

Prostitution is a vice for the same reason that indiscriminate sex is a vice: Sex properly involves a connection of consciousness as well as bodies between two people who genuinely admire one another. Purely physical sex undermines the distinctly human dimension of it (and, besides, there is a good, safe and free alternative to prostitution for those who lack a worthy partner).[141]

Yet neither prostitution nor indiscriminate sex between consenting adults should be legally prohibited because neither violates anyone's rights. Banning some vices is unjust, and banning all vices produces a police state.

Critics of legal prostitution typically make four objections. Prostitution results in physical abuse of women, it spreads sexually transmitted diseases, it corrupts people's character, and it diminishes neighborhoods where it is practiced. None of these objections justifies a prohibition of prostitution.

Just because prostitution is outlawed doesn't mean that it goes away, as news stories about Spitzer and many others demonstrate. What gives rise to physical abuse and disease is precisely the fact that prostitution operates on a black market. On a legal market, both prostitutes and their solicitors would be screened and monitored much more carefully, and prostitutes who suffered abuse would have legal recourse.

---

141 The 2012 film *The Sessions* convinced me that, in some circumstances, prostitution probably is morally permissible. The film involves a mostly-paralyzed man who hires a "sex surrogate." It is based on an article by Mark O'Brien, the subject of the film: "On Seeing A Sex Surrogate," *Sun*, May 1990, issue 174, http://thesunmagazine.org/issues/174/on_seeing_a_sex_surrogate.

Obviously, involuntary prostitution and sexual abuse of children must be outlawed and diligently prevented by the legal system. Making prostitution legal for consenting adults would free up law-enforcement resources to protect children and nonconsenting adults.

The mere presence of something does not corrupt one's character. For example, the fact that most of us live minutes away from liquor stores does not turn us into alcoholics. Nor do we need to mandate the wearing of burkas, as many Muslim regions do (often on pain of physical harm) to prevent men from turning into sexual monsters around women. We do not impose criminal penalties in order to socially discourage adultery, nor do we need them to discourage prostitution.

People are responsible for their own characters. Prohibiting vice (beyond the violation of rights) does not improve people's characters; instead it makes people dependent upon the state for their behavioral guidance, which undermines the rational underpinnings of moral character.

To protect neighborhoods from legal prostitution, some advocate such restrictions as zoning laws. I favor alternatives that are consistent with property rights. For example, voluntary homeowners' associations can rightly prohibit harmful activities. Newspapers can choose not to advertise prostitution. And people are free to socially shun and criticize houses of prostitution.

To preserve a free society, people have to be willing to put up with some things they don't like. Teetotalers must allow bars and liquor stores. Right-wingers must allow socialist bookshops and vice versa. Evangelicals must allow premarital sex, homosexuality, abortion, and dirty movies. We need not condone prostitution, any more than we condone infidelity, to allow that prostitution should be legal.

# Morality and Sanity Demand
# an End to Drug Prohibition

A SET OF GRUESOME PHOTOGRAPHS PUBLISHED by the *Atlantic* in 2012 illustrate the death and destruction caused by the drug policies of the United States. The *Atlantic*'s Alan Taylor summarizes the consequences: "Since Mexico's President Felipe Calderón began an all-out assault on drug cartels in 2006, more than 50,000 people have lost their lives across the country in a nearly-continuous string of shootouts, bombings, and ever-bloodier murders."[142]

To be sure, the brutal members of the drug cartels bear primary responsibility for these murders, perpetrated against rival gangs as well as innocent victims. But U.S.-led policies of drug prohibition establish the conditions in which the drug cartels collect enormous profits selling illegal drugs—profits the cartels pour into weaponry to wage their savage wars for control of the inherently violent black market.

---

142   Alan Taylor, "Mexico's Drug War: 50,000 Dead in 6 Years," *Atlantic*, May 17, 2012, http://www.theatlantic.com/photo/2012/05/mexicos-drug-war-50000-dead-in-6-years/100299/.

U.S. policy bears much of the responsibility for Mexico's horrific drug wars. As the Council on Foreign Relations (CFR) reported, Calderón "launched a massive crackdown against drug trafficking organizations, in conjunction with the United States." In addition to pressuring Mexico politically, "the United States has supplied funding and labor to increase Mexico's institutional capacity to address drug trafficking."[143]

U.S. drug policies result in horrific violence not only in Mexico but also here at home, where drug dealers and drug-dealing gangs murder for drug money day in and day out. Economist Jeffrey Miron estimates in his 2004 book *Drug War Crimes* "that eliminating drug prohibition would reduce homicide in the United States" by at least 25 percent.[144]

What is the rationalization for U.S. interference in Mexico? As CFR points out, "Mexico is a major supplier of heroin to the U.S. market, and the largest foreign supplier of methamphetamine and marijuana." Moreover, around "95 percent of cocaine now travels through Mexico . . . into the United States."

And what consequently travels out of the United States and into Mexico? "The U.S. State Department found that U.S. drug users send between $19 and $29 billion annually into the coffers of Mexican drug cartels."

In other words, the fact that a small minority of Americans choose to harm themselves by abusing drugs is supposed to justify prohibitionist policies that violate Americans' rights to liberty and result in the rise of wealthy and powerful criminal gangsters who murder many thousands of people including Americans every year.

---

143   Brianna Lee, "Mexico's Drug War," Council on Foreign Relations, March 5, 2014, http://www.cfr.org/mexico/mexicos-drug-war/p13689.

144   Jeffrey Miron, *Drug War Crimes* (Oakland, CA: Independent Institute, 2004), p. 51. Miron's estimate is rough; he gives an upper boundary of a 75 percent reduction in homicide. Because violent crime has fallen since the publication of the book even as drug policy has changed somewhat, repealing drug prohibition today perhaps would have less effect on violent crime.

The deadly consequences of drug prohibition flow inexorably from its unjust nature. Prohibition proceeds on the assumption that government should protect adults from the personal consequences of their own decisions and actions. But government should do no such thing. The proper role of government is to protect individual rights by banning physical force from social relationships; thus, government should involve itself with the drug trade only to prevent theft, fraud, and other instances of force.

There is nothing inherently rights-violating in the mere act of consuming drugs (and, indeed, there are perfectly legitimate medical uses for nearly all drugs now declared illegal); thus, government should protect the rights of adults to purchase and consume the substances of their choice.

The fact that the government through its prohibitionist policies systematically violates (rather than protects) individual rights with respect to drug use has given rise to the black market along with the horrific violence inherent therein (not to mention a host of other harms beyond the scope of this essay).

The only sane approach to solving this problem is the moral approach to solving it: Limit government to its proper purpose of protecting individual rights—and thus end drug prohibition.

# Coda

THIS COLLECTION OF ESSAYS HAS COVERED many of the issues relevant today to the struggle for liberty, but certainly it has not covered every important aspect of those issues, and it has left many other important matters (such as "public" education) mostly untouched. The purpose of this compilation has been to offer an insight into the liberal way of thinking (or at least my liberal way) as applied to a slice of contemporary issues. This work is of course a drop in the liberal stream.

The rich tradition and literature of liberalism provide compelling answers to many of the deepest questions about individuals and their rights and proper relation to others, and they offer clear guideposts to most of today's pressing policy issues. Yet liberalism remains a work in progress; certainly as a liberal I cannot answer to my own satisfaction a variety of important questions.

Here are some of the key questions facing modern liberals:

- What is the deepest moral basis of individualism, the idea that individuals properly pursue their own life and values and have a moral right to do so? Older "natural law" arguments are flimsy. Ayn Rand has done some groundbreaking work in this area, yet her idea that all of a person's proper values ultimately support that person's survival cannot, I believe, be sustained. I think the answer lies in a somewhat different development of Aristotle's ethics than what Rand offers, focusing on an ultimate moral end which is the sum total of a person's integrated values. (I plan to flesh out this theory at some point.)

- What is the full basis and nature of individual rights? Again the liberal tradition has made great strides, yet many problems remain. For example, what exactly is the proper limit of contracts or scope of intellectual property? Modern conservatives offer no help; typically they parrot the idea that "rights come from God," with no evidence for their claims, little explanation for what these rights are, and no reason to take these rights seriously. Ayn Rand recognizes the crucial point that rights enable a person to act on his judgment in pursuit of his life and values; many details of a full theory of rights remain to be worked out or revisited.

- What is the full nature of proper government? Constitutional republicanism is the heart of liberal governance, I have claimed. But, ideally, how does such a government operate? How does it recognize citizenship—an especially important issue in the context of immigration—and what is the proper scope of citizen participation in governance? How does government properly interact with non-citizens at home and with citizens and non-citizens abroad? This is an especially thorny problem in the age of terrorism.

- Crucially, how is government properly financed? I believe that, ultimately, government should not tax people—that is, take their money by force. But then how is it to operate? And is it true that government necessarily violates people's rights by taxing them? Of course the anarchists want to do away with taxes, but they also want to do away with government. Does proper morality demand the abolition of taxation, and, if so, what is the workable alternative? Various people have done some good work along these lines; more such work is needed.

- Regarding foreign policy, can people both maintain a rights-respecting government at home and take paramilitary action, if they wish, to assist people elsewhere suffering under oppression and tyranny? If so, should government be involved in such action, and (if so) under what circumstances? If citizens act outside of government, how should a rights-respecting government interact with extra-governmental efforts to intervene in foreign affairs, given that such efforts may well embroil a nation in conflict?

- How should government deal with torts involving peoples of different nations? The prominent example today is climate change. So far, it seems (to me at least) that the luke-warmists are correct and the climate catastrophists are wrong. But even if carbon (and other) emissions harm only some parties in moderate ways, is that not sufficient for government to intervene in some way? If so, how should government intervene? My tentative idea is that government should, if anything, enforce compensation of parties suffering objectively proved harm—but this is undeveloped. Hypothetically, what if some sort of widespread activity did cumulatively cause widespread harm? I'm convinced that subsidies and taxes are bad ways to approach such problems, but I'm not sure what is the right way.

- How, specifically, should government deal with criminals? It should try to stop them when possible, obviously, and it should take action against them. The difficulty is in the details. The prison model has long been the norm, but modern prisons clearly are a disaster in many respects, often featuring arbitrary sentences, violent assaults and other inhumane treatment, and the opposite of rehabilitative influences. I think future generations will view our prisons much as we view the dreadful mental institutions of eras past. But how should prisons be reformed, and when should they be used? What positive role, if any, should government play in rehabilitating criminals?

How should government interact with private organizations regarding the treatment of criminals?

- How far should government go to protect children? I regard any hitting of a child (including spanking) as wrong, but when should it be regarded as a rights violation? I oppose circumcision (absent specific medical reason), but should it be banned? Generally, liberal societies have moved toward greater protection of children, and I think that's good, but what are the appropriate limits of government action? And under what circumstances should government take children from parents or facilitate private groups in taking such action?

- Is there any role for government to play regarding abortion? The position I have staked out is that a woman has a moral right to get an abortion at any time during pregnancy. But obviously late-term abortions raise important moral issues, especially when there is no apparent medical need. Is there any room at all for a liberal government to intervene in this area? I'd like to see more work here.

- Does government play any proper role in protecting animals (beyond protecting the rights of animal owners)? My answer has long been no, but I want to think through the issue again. Most people would be horrified at the possibility of legalizing the brutal torture of dogs, for example. The horrific treatment of many animals in "factory farms" prompts many people to call for reforms—but should such reforms involve government? This is a question with far-reaching implications regarding the liberal theory of rights and the theory of rights-respecting government. If government protects animals, then what else might it do besides protect people's rights?

I have good leads in answering such questions, but my answers to many of these thorny questions are tentative and incomplete. Liberals have a lot of work to do to develop their underlying theories of ethics and rights and to apply those theories to the pressing issues of the day. Liberalism is in some respects a destination, but in important respects it is a continual journey.

Yet we should not lose sight of just how far liberalism has come. Slavery, for example, once was almost universally accepted as the norm. Not too many decades ago, it was deeply controversial. Then, in almost an instant historically speaking, it was outlawed by several of the most prominent governments on earth. That is extraordinary. Or consider the rights of homosexuals—not too long ago police in the United States harassed gay people; today, homosexuals can marry on the same terms as heterosexuals. In these and many other ways, liberalism has made great strides.

Liberalism is a project both of refining the theory of individual rights and of applying that theory to the pressing problems of the day. The fact that liberals still have some work to do to refine their theory of rights in no way detracts from the great strides that liberals have made to date. The fact that liberals cannot definitively answer every question does not mean that liberals cannot definitively answer many important questions. Slavery is wrong. Government discrimination against minority groups is wrong. Seizing the wealth belonging to one person to enrich another person is wrong. Forcibly preventing a person from pursuing his values for no good reason is wrong. Locking people in metal cages—or otherwise inflicting harm on them— when they violate no one's rights is wrong. Advancing a rights-respecting society and a rights-respecting government is right.

In some regions, liberalism never found much of a foothold; in others, it is in retreat if not completely beaten back—as the slaves of Islamic State and the victims of racist warlords and theocratic totalitarians would attest. In the relatively liberal United States, such things as runaway government spending, mass surveillance, and widespread antipathy to freedom of speech threaten to reverse some of the hard-fought liberal advances our society has made.

Liberalism is hard. It is hard to know what are the deepest philosophic justifications for liberalism, and it is hard to apply liberal insights to messy contemporary politics. Yet there is no cause more worthy, for liberalism either subsumes other important human-advancing causes or helps enable their progress.

The advances of liberalism didn't "just happen"; they were not inevitable; they were the victories of the hard work of liberal thinkers and activists. And if we do not keep moving the liberal tradition forward, our society will become less liberal, less open, less prosperous, more oppressive.

Today some of us are relatively free. Yet no one on earth lives in a fully free and liberal society, and some people live under brutal oppression. The lack of liberty around the world is a human tragedy and a moral atrocity. Not only is injustice anywhere a threat to justice everywhere, as liberals have always recognized, but oppression throttles or destroys vast numbers of lives and prevents countless individuals from joining (or fully joining) the global community of traders. To the degree that others suffer injustice, each of us is diminished. We owe it to ourselves at least to create a beacon of liberty in our own land and to encourage people elsewhere to follow.

We hold these truths, as demonstrable if not self-evident, that all people are equal in their moral rights to life, liberty, property, and the pursuit of happiness. That is the liberal promise and the liberal demand. Now it is up to each of us to help fulfill that promise.

# Acknowledgements

MY WIFE JENNIFER ARMSTRONG proofread the material, designed the cover and text, and generally helped to facilitate this work. Sharon Armstrong also helped with proofreading. Linn Armstrong contributed as coauthor to two of the pieces in this volume, as indicated below. Most of the essays in this compilation originally were published by the *Objective Standard* (see below), which retains copyright to those essays; they appear here by agreement. Craig Biddle, that journal's editor and publisher, played an important role in editing those pieces. Of course, none of the people I've associated with or learned from bears any responsibility for my statements or conclusions.

# Publication Notes

To FACILITATE STANDARDIZED CITATIONS of this book, ebook editions include subscripted, bracketed numbers corresponding to the beginning of pages in the print edition. (The ebook is free-flowing, so of course a bracketed number may appear anywhere on a display screen.)

The print edition uses footnotes, so each note appears at the bottom of the page on which its note marker appears (and no note splits between pages). In ebook editions, the notes appear together near the end, and hyperlinks shuttle between note markers and notes. To reduce the need to flip pages, each note includes all of the relevant citation information, except where "ibid." or an abbreviated citation could be substituted on the same printed page.

Following are details of the original publication of the essays contained in this volume; all but the lead essay and the coda were published previously. The previously published essays were edited for this volume, usually lightly but in a few cases heavily. Some of the titles have been changed.

Ari Armstrong, "The Irrationality of Neil deGrasse Tyson's Rationalia," AriArmstrong.com, August 11, 2016, http://ariarmstrong.com/2016/08/the-irrationality-of-neil-degrasse-tysons-rationalia/.

Ari Armstrong, "Sam Harris's Failure to Formulate a Scientific Morality," *Objective Standard*, Winter 2012, vol. 7, no. 4, https://www.theobjectivestandard.com/issues/2012-winter/sam-harris-unscientific-morality/.

Ari Armstrong, "'You Didn't Build That'—Obama's Ode to Envy," *Objective Standard*, July 20, 2012, https://www.theobjectivestandard.com/2012/07/you-didnt-build-that-obamas-ode-to-envy/.

Ari Armstrong, "The Justice of Income Inequality Under Capitalism," *Objective Standard*, October 19, 2011, https://www.theobjectivestandard.com/2011/10/the-justice-of-income-inequality-under-capitalism/.

Ari Armstrong, "Egalitarianism versus Rational Morality on Income Inequality," *Objective Standard*, May 24, 2014, https://www.theobjectivestandard.com/2014/05/egalitarianism-vs-rational-morality-income-inequality/.

Ari Armstrong, "Watkins and Brook Offer Book Challenging Inequality Narrative," AriArmstrong.com, March 23, 2016, http://ariarmstrong.com/2016/03/watkins-and-brook-return-with-book-challenging-inequality-narrative/.

Ari Armstrong, "Responsibility & Luck" (Review), *Objective Standard*, Spring 2014, vol. 9, no. 1, https://www.theobjectivestandard.com/issues/2014-spring/review-responsibility-luck-by-diana-hsieh/.

Ari Armstrong, "A Parable for Thomas Piketty," *Objective Standard*, May 6, 2015, https://www.theobjectivestandard.com/2015/05/a-parable-for-thomas-piketty/.

Ari Armstrong, "Contra Occupiers, Profits Embody Justice," *Objective Standard*, December 2, 2011, https://www.theobjectivestandard.com/2011/12/contra-occupiers-profits-embody-justice/.

Ari Armstrong, "Brook and Watkins Spark Free Market Revolution," *Objective Standard*, Fall 2012, vol. 7, no. 3, https://www.theobjectivestandard.com/issues/2012-fall/review-free-market-revolution/.

Ari Armstrong, "The Fruits of Capitalism Are All Around Us," *Objective Standard*, March 3, 2013, https://www.theobjectivestandard.com/2013/03/the-fruits-of-capitalism-are-all-around-us/.

Ari Armstrong, "A Lesson On Civil Disobedience and Censorship," *Complete Colorado*, October 2, 2014, http://completecolorado.com/pagetwo/2014/10/02/a-lesson-on-censorship-and-civil-disobedience-for-jeffco-students-teachers-and-observers/.

Ari Armstrong, "When Politics Corrupts Money," *Objective Standard*, October 6, 2012, https://www.theobjectivestandard.com/2012/10/when-politics-corrupts-money/.

Ari Armstrong, "Why Forcibly Limiting Campaign Spending is Censorship—And Why it Matters," *Objective Standard*, October 14, 2012, https://www.theobjectivestandard.com/2012/10/why-forcibly-limiting-campaign-spending-is-censorship/.

Ari Armstrong, "The Egalitarian Assault on Free Speech," *Objective Standard*, October 18, 2012, https://www.theobjectivestandard.com/2012/10/the-egalitarian-assault-on-free-speech/.

Ari Armstrong and Linn Armstrong, "Colorado's Campaign Laws Throw Common Sense Out the Window," *Grand Junction Free Press*, May 13, 2011, http://ariarmstrong.com/2011/05/colorados-campaign-laws-throw-common-sense-out-the-window/.

Ari Armstrong, "Colorado Judge: Today's 'Tom Paine's Pamphlet' Is Protected Speech," *Objective Standard*, October 12, 2014, https://www.theobjectivestandard .com/2014/10/colorado-judge-todays-tom-paines-pamphlet-protected-speech/.

Ari Armstrong, "After the Welfare State" (Review), *Objective Standard*, Summer 2013, vol. 8, no. 2, https://www.theobjectivestandard.com/issues/2013-summer/ after-the-welfare-state/.

Ari Armstrong, "The Moral Integrity of Condemning Social Security While Collecting It," *Objective Standard*, November 3, 2012, https://www.theobjectivestandard.com/ 2012/11/the-moral-integrity-of-condemning-social-security-while-collecting-it/.

Ari Armstrong and Linn Armstrong, "Nation Needs Shared Liberty, Not Sacrifice," *Grand Junction Free Press*, September 2, 2011, http://ariarmstrong.com/2011/09/ nation-needs-shared-liberty-not-sacrifice/.

Ari Armstrong, "The Crucial Distinction Between Subsidies and Tax Cuts," *Objective Standard*, November 23, 2012, https://www.theobjectivestandard.com/2012/11/ the-crucial-distinction-between-subsidies-and-tax-cuts/.

Ari Armstrong, "The Moral Case Against Minimum Wage Laws," AriArmstrong.com, http://ariarmstrong.com/2016/09/the-moral-case-against-minimum-wage-laws/.

Ari Armstrong, "The Morality of Unequal Pay for Unequal Work," *Objective Standard*, June 11, 2012, https://www.theobjectivestandard.com/2012/06/the -morality-of-unequal-pay-for-unequal-work/.

Ari Armstrong, "After Hobby Lobby Ruling, How About Government Protect the Rights of Everyone?," *Objective Standard*, July 6, 2014, https://www.theobjectivestandard .com/2014/07/hobby-lobby-ruling-government-protect-rights-everyone/.

Ari Armstrong, "On the Right Not to Bake a Cake," *Objective Standard*, June 4, 2014, https://www.theobjectivestandard.com/2014/06/right-bake-cake/.

Ari Armstrong, "No, Denver Post, Businessmen Should Never 'Put Moral Judgments Aside,'" *Objective Standard*, June 6, 2014, https://www.theobjectivestandard .com/2014/06/denver-post-businessmen-never-put-moral-judgments-aside/.

Ari Armstrong, "Religious Freedom Laws vs. Equal Protection of Rights," *Objective Standard*, April 3, 2015, https://www.theobjectivestandard.com/2015/04/religious -freedom-laws-vs-equal-protection-of-rights/.

Ari Armstrong, "Rational Morality Requires Amnesty for Rights-Respecting Illegal Immigrants," *Objective Standard*, July 2, 2014, https://www.theobjectivestandard .com/2014/07/rational-morality-requires-amnesty-rights-respecting-illegal -immigrants/.

Ari Armstrong, "Myths and Facts about a Rights-Respecting Immigration Policy," *Objective Standard*, July 20, 2014, https://www.theobjectivestandard.com/2014/07/ myths-facts-rights-respecting-immigration-policy/.

Ari Armstrong, "Government Destroys Buckyballs, Assaults the Mind," *Objective Standard*, December 14, 2012, https://www.theobjectivestandard.com/2012/12/government-destroys-buckyballs-assaults-the-mind/.

Ari Armstrong, "Should Prostitution Be Legal?," *Rocky Mountain News*, March 15, 2008, https://web.archive.org/web/20080321173506/http://www.rockymountainnews.com/news/2008/mar/15/should-prostitution-be-legal/.

Ari Armstrong, "Morality and Sanity Demand an End to Drug Prohibition," *Objective Standard*, June 4, 2012, https://www.theobjectivestandard.com/2012/06/morality-and-sanity-demand-an-end-to-drug-prohibition/.

# Keep in Touch

PLEASE JOIN my email list via my web page at AriArmstrong.com.

On Facebook, follow me at
https://www.facebook.com/AriArmstrongWriter/.

My Twitter handle is ariarmstrong.

You can help support my work, and get exclusive content, via my
Patreon account at https://www.patreon.com/ariarmstrong/.

# Index

·

www.ingramcontent.com/pod-product-compliance
Lightning Source LLC
Chambersburg PA
CBHW070304290326
41930CB00040B/2076